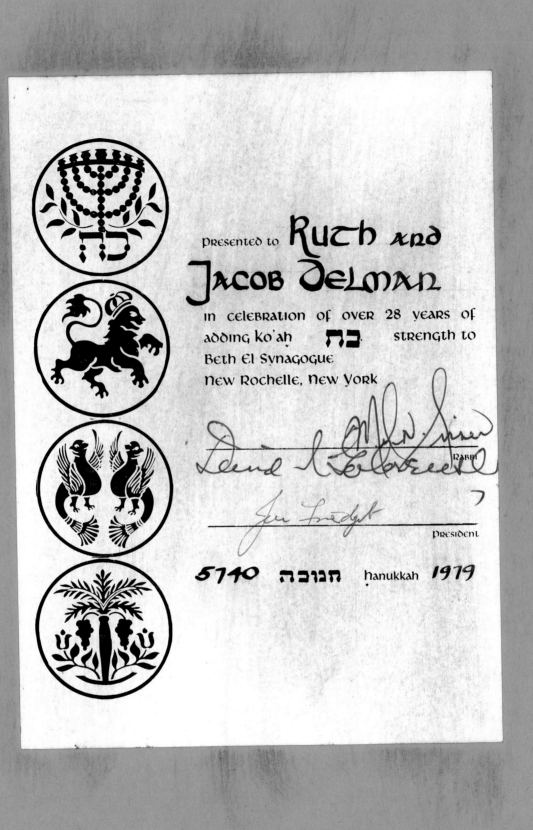

PRESENTED TO **RUTH AND JACOB DELMAN**

IN CELEBRATION OF OVER 28 YEARS OF
adding ko'aḥ **כֹּחַ** strength to
Beth El Synagogue
New Rochelle, New York

RABBI

PRESIDENT

5740 חנוכה ḥanukkah 1979

LET THEM MAKE ME A
SANCTUARY

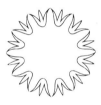

LET THEM MAKE ME A

A Contemporary American Synagogue

Inspired by the Art of Ancient Israel

SANCTUARY

by STANLEY IRVING BATKIN

BEHRMAN HOUSE INC. *New York, New York*

The title of this book, LET THEM MAKE ME A SANCTUARY,
is taken from *Exodus 25:8*

Library of Congress Cataloging in Publication Data

Batkin, Stanley I   1914–
  Let them make me a sanctuary.

  Includes index.
  1. Beth-El Synagogue, New Rochelle, N. Y.
2. Synagogue architecture—United States. 3. Jews in New Rochelle, N.Y.
I. Title.
NA5235.N538B37   726'.3'0947277   78–16933
ISBN 0–87441–316–8

Published by Behrman House, Inc., 1261 Broadway, New York, N.Y. 10001
Manufactured in the United States of America

To my parents and grandparents for their inspiration;

to my darling wife, Selma;

to my children and grandchildren as a legacy.

CONTENTS

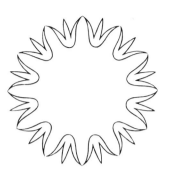

PHOTOGRAPHERS:

Malcolm Varon   *New York, New York*

David Franzen   *Katonah, New York*

Stanley I. Batkin   *New Rochelle, New York*

COLOR NEGATIVES:

Beck Engraving Co. Inc.   *Philadelphia, Pennsylvania*

Perma Plate   *South Hackensack, New Jersey*

Swan Engraving Company   *Bridgeport, Connecticut*

COLOR PRINTING:

Metro Litho Graving Co. Inc.   *Moonachie, New Jersey*

LIST OF COLOR PLATES

BUT CAN GOD INDEED DWELL ON EARTH? HEAVEN ITSELF, THE HIGHEST HEAVEN, CANNOT CONTAIN THEE; HOW MUCH LESS THIS HOUSE THAT I HAVE BUILT! YET ATTEND TO THE PRAYER AND THE SUPPLICATION OF THY SERVANT . . . HEAR THE PRAYER OR SUPPLICATION OF EVERY MAN AMONG THY PEOPLE, ISRAEL . . . AS EACH ONE, PROMPTED BY THE REMORSE OF HIS OWN HEART, SPREADS OUT HIS HANDS TOWARD THIS HOUSE. . . . THE FOREIGNER, TOO, THE MAN WHO DOES NOT BELONG TO THY PEOPLE, ISRAEL, RESPOND TO THE CALL WHICH THE FOREIGNER MAKES TO THEE.

—*King Solomon's Prayer at the Dedication of His Temple, 954 B.C.E. (I Kings 8)*

FOREWORD

Most great cultures—Babylonian, Egyptian, Greek, Roman, that of the Gothic Era and of the Renaissance—incorporated art into their lives largely in public and religious buildings. This was a way of bringing the art of the time into everyday use and appreciation. Art embellished people's lives.

With the Industrial Revolution, this presence of art began to lose its human qualities, and only rarely was there a continuity of art and architecture planned together as part of culture.

Beth El Synagogue of New Rochelle, New York, is an outstanding example of the rebirth of the concept of art and architecture as one. As its architect, I look back with pride and satisfaction. I had a client who directed art incorporation from the inception—ceramic murals, stained glass, bas-reliefs, sculptures—as well as a specially designed ark, menorah, and furnishings, all toward a harmonious whole.

Stanley Batkin's scholarly, dedicated approach complemented our architectural endeavors to create a sanctuary and other areas that reflect both the religious history of our people and its contemporary life.

This book is a testament to the enlightenment of the people who made it possible. The joy lies with the beholder of this book and of this building.

EDGAR TAFEL, *Architect*

CHRONOLOGY

Beth El Synagogue is located in New Rochelle, New York, a suburban city in Westchester County, just north of New York City. Westchester has a population of approximately one million people, of whom 135,000 are Jews. Eighteen percent of these Jewish people live in New Rochelle. This city, founded in 1688 by Huguenots escaping religious persecution in France, became a haven for Jewish settlers seeking religious freedom in the early 1700s. The earliest recorded Jewish birth in New Rochelle was that of David Hays in 1732. Hays later served in Washington's army and helped to supply the American troops.

Jewish religious services in New Rochelle were held first in homes and later in the synagogues of neighboring towns. During the wave of emigration from Eastern Europe in the 1880s and 1890s, several hundred additional Jews found their way to New Rochelle. However, it was not until the beginning of the twentieth century that the first Jewish house of worship was built in New Rochelle.

The Orthodox synagogue Anshe Sholom opened its doors in 1904 and was followed in 1908 by Temple Israel, the Reform congregation. Beth El Synagogue, originally known as the Hebrew Institute, was started in 1909 by fifty families of the Conservative leaning. Its objectives were "to foster, encourage, promote, induce, and advance the study of the Hebrew language and its literature."

During the early 1900s, Beth El occupied eight successive rented premises. After World War I, the Jewish population had so increased that the members felt it necessary to build a permanent home. In 1923 a lot was purchased for the building of a synagogue at 31 Union Avenue.

In March 1927, the 202 member families gathered together in the new building for the first time.

During the 1940s the membership rose to about 350 families. Dr. David I. Golovensky became Beth El's spiritual leader in 1946, and in 1949 Beth El merged with the newly formed North End Synagogue. A few months later, in October 1949, four and one-half acres were purchased at Northfield Road and North Avenue in the northern section of the city for the purpose of building a community center and eventually a sanctuary.

The community center portion was dedicated in 1957; the school wing, containing fourteen classrooms, a school auditorium, library, study rooms, and offices, in 1961. Both sections were designed by Charles R. Meyers and Herbert Phillips. The contractor was the Blitman Construction Corp.

The building of the synagogue was authorized by the board of trustees in 1966; Edgar Tafel was engaged as the architect in November 1967; and ground was broken for the building in February 1969. The first High Holy Day services were conducted in the new sanctuary in 1970, and on the seventh of Iyar, 5731 (May 2, 1971), the synagogue was dedicated. The builders were Cuzzi Bros. & Singer Inc. The synagogue wing included the main sanctuary, lobbies, reception room, gift shop, bridal room, mothers' and infants' room, Sukkah garden, two chapels, library, museum, and numerous offices.

LET THEM MAKE ME A
SANCTUARY

THE BUILDING OF A SYNAGOGUE CENTER

THIS IS NONE OTHER THAN THE HOUSE OF GOD:
THIS IS THE GATE OF HEAVEN.
                                    —*Genesis 28:17*

Two of the earliest recollections of my childhood are of my grandfather and father taking active leadership roles in the founding and building of their respective synagogues. I remember a weekend spent with my grandparents, Rose and Michael Tenzer, during the summer of 1923, when the founding meeting of the Yeshiva of Crown Heights, Brooklyn, New York, was held in their home. From this meeting an institution of religion and learning grew to greatness. Also indelibly written in my memory is the meeting on May 1, 1924, when my father and nine other men founded the East Midwood Jewish Center of Brooklyn, New York. These events impressed me beyond measure, and I was inspired to continue in the noble tradition of my family. I always felt that one day I would have the opportunity to take an active role in building a House of Worship.

The opportunity came after I moved my family to New Rochelle, New York, in 1946. We joined Beth El Synagogue, the nearest Conservative institution, located several miles from our home. While at High Holy Day services there, it soon became clear to me and to a neighbor, Herman J. Greenhut, that the facilities were very limited and unable to serve the ever-increasing number of families in the northern end of the city. On May 5, 1949, therefore, I called a meeting in my home to explore the possibility of forming a new synagogue. In response to my invitation to ten men, eight were present: Isadore and Seymour Baum, Benjamin Charnas, Morris Golub, Dr. Sanford Goodfriend, Herman J. Greenhut, Maxwell James, and Rabbi Harry Katchen of the Jewish Theological Seminary of America.

Within several weeks the response to invitations to our meetings was so great that we were well on our way to establishing a new synagogue. Two neighbors and friends, Ben Charnas and Harold Drimmer, shared with me the rotating chairmanship of the meetings. Various committees were formed, and plans were made for High Holy Day services in the fall. However, when Beth El's leadership learned of our intentions, they insisted that we merge with them, with the agreement that the combined institution would build new facilities uptown. Although we complied with their wishes, many of us did so reluctantly, believing that two institutions would better serve the geographically large community.

When the two congregations merged in 1949, I was given the overall responsibility for fund-raising and building the proposed complex in the North End. During the first two stages of the construction program, which involved the center building and the school wing, I was ably assisted by Alfred Goldstein, a civil engineer now in the real estate business, who served as chairman of the building committee. As construction of these areas progressed I was already planning the main sanctuary, still many years in the future. I set out to educate myself and otherwise prepare for the great undertaking that lay ahead. For the next two decades I read extensively, traveled in Europe, Israel, and at home, met and held discussions with artists and scholars, and formulated many ideas for future use. When, in 1966, the time came to build the sanctuary, I felt prepared to undertake the chairmanship of the committee to design and construct the sanctuary.

The entire congregation was invited to join our committee, and eighty members volunteered. Our first activity was a series of visits to other synagogues. These trips, led by Dr. Abraham Geffen, oriented the committee and laid the path for the determination of our goals. From November 1966 to the spring of 1967, we spent seven Sundays, visiting eight different synagogues each day, in New Jersey, Pennsylvania, Long Island, Westchester, and Connecticut. Additional trips to areas that were farther away, such as Boston and Baltimore, were made in smaller groups, and reports were also brought in from individual visitors to synagogues throughout the world.

Several report meetings were held to analyze the places visited, and an accord of ideas was reached. The consensus of our members reflected a desire to achieve a functional building, contemporary in design and structure, expressive of the age in which we live, and utilizing the most advanced material and building technology available.

We further sought to incorporate evidence of our great Judaic heritage in the building, and to provide decorations for it that would reflect traditional aspects of our past. During our trips to synagogues, we sought to learn from the experience of others. We discussed the positive and negative aspects of each building, as well as any problems encountered by members and staff of the various congregations. After much consideration we established optimum dimensions for various components of the sanctuary, such as bimah, aisles, and seating.

From our visits, we listed four architects whose buildings we admired. Eight additional architects, whom we either sought out or who were recommended to us, were added to our list. The committee then interviewed the twelve architects, and narrowed the list down to four, inviting these people to return for a more detailed discussion. The two leading candidates came from the group whose buildings we had originally admired. Finally, we decided on Edgar Tafel of New York—based on his previous work, the quality of his staff, his careful attention to detail, and his clients' satisfaction.

EDGAR TAFEL, THE ARCHITECT

Edgar Tafel, born in New York City, studied architecture at New York University, then trained for nine years under Frank Lloyd Wright at the Taliesin Fellowship. During his apprenticeship, he became a senior and was job architect for such noted buildings as Fallingwater and the Johnson Wax Building.

After World War II, Mr. Tafel established his office in New York City, designing over sixty custom homes and many religious buildings, including three temples, the Protestant Chapel at Kennedy Airport, and several New York churches. He has master-planned three colleges as well, and designed the State University College at Geneseo, New York, and York College, Queens, New York.

Mr. Tafel has been active in the American Institute of Architects, chairing many committees and serving on its executive committee. He has lectured widely for the U.S. Information Agency in England, India, the Netherlands, and Israel, both on his own work and on that of Frank Lloyd Wright. He has received many prizes, and his works have been reported in all the architectural magazines in the United States as well as several publications in England.

As background material to add to Mr. Tafel's library, I supplied him with a few dozen books on synagogues, the twelve-volume *Jewish Encyclopedia* of 1907, a list of Rabbi Golovensky's suggestions, a list of selected passages I had garnered from the Hertz *Humash*, a description of King Solomon's Temple by Harry Gingold, one of our committee members, and considerable other pertinent material.

A week before the dedication of the synagogue, Mr. Tafel would write to the Beth El Congregation:

Edgar Tafel

*Beth El Synagogue
Construction, 1968*

The design of Beth El was a deep challenge—to add to an existing structure a sanctuary that would transcend time and space. . . . The plan layout was predicated on the existing circulation patterns as was the relationship of the new sanctuary and reception hall to the existing social hall. With the committee, I reviewed many plans and buildings to arrive at the most appropriate plan.

In order to create a spiritual aura, the sanctuary was conceived basically as a windowless space. We intentionally decided on small amounts of stained glass and skylite to give direction and focus to the bimah area. The exterior massive walls, capped by a limestone cornice, clearly articulate this portion of the building complex. In these ways, I feel that a successful and significant design solution has been achieved. This is truly a joint effort of concept, design, and execution.

During the year after Mr. Tafel was chosen, there were nightly and weekend meetings with my devoted cochairman Dan Locitzer, Director of Development for the city of New Rochelle, and Jack Rosen, a real estate developer and builder. We also held weekly meetings with the architect and report meetings with the larger committee. Plans for a layout and complete foundation were completed in about a year. The foundation contract was placed separately as a spur to our fund-raising activities. We continued with our planning.

The Beth El Building Committee consisted of many talented and knowledgeable persons with diverse opinions, all pressed with much force and conviction. As an obliging architect felt compelled to respond at length to each suggestion, our decision-making ability was seriously impeded. A delay of six months developed while our large committee debated the merits of the façade renderings, particularly the crown of the roof. Since this was a crucial period of rising prices, the delay was responsible for the loss of a six-figure sum in increased building costs. It became apparent to me that a small committee of three, backed by ten specialists, could do the major work. These three would use the larger committee for advice, approval, or rejection, avoiding the lengthy debates over intricate details. By proceeding on this basis, we eliminated a substantial portion of our problems. The balance of the plans was ready for contract bidding six months later.

While work proceeded on the building plans, I organized my list of artistic projects and assigned them to particular structural areas. From twenty years of research I had available some thirty ideas for works of art, and had assembled the names of hundreds of artists who might be able to implement these ideas. The artists were grouped by their mode of expression and by their style. I outlined the proposed works of art on separate fact sheets with background material, historical facts, and scholarly descriptive studies commissioned by us. Rabbi Golovensky was most helpful in his advice on these matters. Edgar Tafel and his aides were very supportive in their areas of professional expertise. They provided blueprints of each area, sat in on discussions, coordinated installations, and designed and produced finished drawings for several items, such as pulpit furniture and dignitary seats.

My list of artists had been assembled from a variety of sources— including recommendations made by the United Synagogue of America and the Union of American Hebrew Congregations, works of art I had seen in various synagogues and museums, articles in art magazines, and suggestions from individuals. Several of my projected ideas, such as the Wall of the Martyrs and the weekly portion of the Torah, were only concepts in my mind. I needed artists to bring these dreams to realization. There was a slow and careful period of matching artists to plans, of continuing to search for artists who could express my ideas in a suitable medium at or near my budget figures. While the budget presented a problem in many areas, precluding the use of certain artists, I never compromised my high ideals in the selection of the talent.

The two decades of preparation witnessed my gradual and steady immersion in the field of art and in study of the Bible, the Commentaries, and related literature. There were also visits to museums and synagogues, and encounters with artists in this country, Israel, and Europe. Influenced by the Hasidic concept of a bit of God in everything, I strove to pick and choose each object that would be in the synagogue for its meaning and its special holiness. In addition I sought to commission Israeli artists whenever possible, and to have them create works based on authentic historical finds of ancient Israel.

It was a very rewarding time for me personally, opening new vistas and expanding my field of activities. I became a collector of art, books, glass, silver, and ritual objects.

This book is an account of the history, development, and realization of the art in the synagogue, with an explanation of the special quality of each of the many objects now enshrined in Beth El Synagogue of New Rochelle.

Edgar Tafel's rendering,
Beth El Synagogue

THE FAÇADE

The façade of Beth El Synagogue features a gold menorah, crowning the biblical Ten Commandments, and creating a soaring, strong impression. The Ten Commandments, Israel's greatest contribution to the moral development of the world, here symbolize the foundation of Western civilization, particularly its religious and moral code. The menorah is meant to act as a beacon to members of the Jewish faith.

This menorah was inspired by a stone carving unearthed at an ancient synagogue site in Israel. It was stylized at my request and unfortunately lost most of its resemblance to the original. The vertical limestone panel in which the menorah is cast was designed as a vehicle to show both the menorah and the Ten Commandments in their best light.

The pilasters of the exterior walls give strength in a fortified appearance. A special brick of dark, earthy, desert colors was manufactured to our specifications. The limestone cornice of the building simulates elements that appear in reproductions of King Solomon's Temple. The front of the building has a park setting with walks, benches, and a fountain with a pool. This pool was named the Pool of Siloam, after the ancient pool that supplied water to the Temple of King Solomon. The pools are still in Jerusalem, and every year, on the evening of the first day of Sukkot, Simhat Beit HaSho'evah, water-drawing festivities occur. The president of Israel and the chief rabbis usually lead the gatherings, and the participants join in group singing and dancing.

Specifications for the façade lettering

THE GREAT SANCTUARY

LET THEM MAKE ME A SANCTUARY,
THAT I MAY DWELL AMONG THEM.
—*Exodus 25:8*

The great sanctuary, lending itself to reverence and spirituality, is a place where each individual can make quiet yet eloquent communication with his Maker. The decorative aspects are restrained and understated. A serene, contemplative beauty is discernible as one enters this house of worship. The side walls are stark gray, with ten ceramic murals appearing to be a view of the exterior from clear windows. The magnificent murals are muted in appearance and yet of rare beauty.

The ark is the focus of attention. Everything in the sanctuary serves to frame the ark, to enhance the ark, to guide the eye to the ark, but never to compete with or detract from it. The shape of the brilliant stained-glass windows is deliberately narrow so as not to detract from the ark. The ark is complemented by the ancient eternal light and the single menorah, acting as an introduction to the bimah.

THE BIMAH

The bimah area is a 56-foot-wide expanse creating a oneness with the congregation and a spacious setting directing the attention of the worshipper to the ark. The level of the bimah is just sufficiently high so that the services can be viewed properly. The bimah is connected to the main floor by five steps running the entire width of the sanctuary.

Western Wall and Bema Wall

The great ark for our sanctuary was designed by Edgar Tafel.

On a visit to Copenhagen, Denmark, I had been struck by the beauty of the ark in the main synagogue there, and in particular by the reverential phrases inscribed on it. The caretaker told me the story of the Nazi occupation, when the Torahs and silver ornaments normally stored in the ark were hidden for the duration of World War II in a church diagonally across the street. The synagogue was redecorated by the Danish government after the war, with the king in attendance at the first service. I photographed and copied the Hebrew phrases on both the exterior and interior of the ark, so that they could be used in the Beth El ark. I chose these phrases not only for their beauty but also as a tribute to the Kingdom of Denmark, which alone among the states of Europe rescued its Jewish citizens during the Nazi Holocaust.

Mr. Tafel's design for the crown of our ark simulates renderings of King Solomon's Temple: "Make upon it a crown of gold." [1] The crown includes the legend: *Shiviti adonai lenegdi tamid* ("I place the Lord before me at all times"), taken from Psalm 16:8.

The interior of the ark has the *Shema*, the affirmation of our faith. Even the script was carefully chosen: it is one used exclusively for writing on parchments in the Torah, tefillin, and mezuzot. The embellishments above some of the letters are called *Tagin*, single or triple, and are used exclusively on those letters as indicated; they derive from a twelfth century Egyptian alphabet.

The colored stones on the doors and body of the ark represent the stones of the Twelve Tribes mentioned in the Bible. [2] The main body and doors of the ark are gold-anodized aluminum. There are about four thousand chunks of translucent colored polyester glass in this body. The ark of King Solomon's Temple was made of wood and was gold-plated so that it "shone and glistened." [3]

The base of the ark is bronze, with the statement: "This is the Torah proclaimed by Moses to the children of Israel at the command of the Lord." [4]

The shape of the ark, oblong with elliptical ends, presented a budgetary problem in its implementation. The plans called for tambourine doors, parting in the center and sliding off to each side, curving inside the side walls. To overcome the excessive cost, I designed two sets of two doors, each on recessed tracks. Each set slides behind the straight remaining front portion of the ark, creating three levels of

[1] Ex. 25:11.
[2] Ex. 28:17–20.
[3] Jerusalem Talmud, Shekalim 6:1.
[4] Deut. 4:44.

glass walls. The cutting of the aluminum walls to hold the thousands of polyester chunks led to another cost problem. Here I proposed die-cutting irregular pieces of aluminum, 15 by 22 inches, and fitting them together so that the pattern of glass would be viewed as an overall design rather than pieced elements. These successful solutions saved the designer's artistic conception. The first solution was based on the principle of elevator doors; the second, on the layout pattern used in the preparation of folding carton dies.

ETERNAL LIGHT

The eternal light is a rare antique designed many centuries ago by an unknown skilled artisan who was able to fuse silver, copper, and brass through a technique now all but lost.

I purchased the lamp from Peter Ehrenthal, one of the foremost Judaica dealers in New York, who had purchased it from a source in the Near East. This unique and priceless treasure hung for many centuries in a synagogue in Damascus, Syria. The artist engrossed in silver on the eternal light phrases from the Bible, chosen for their beauty and pertinence. I have found them to be especially inspirational.

On the top level is inscribed: *Vayishama kol sason ve-simhah* ("There will be heard the voice of joy and of gladness"). This phrase, part of which is found in the last of the wedding blessings, is a paraphrase of Jeremiah 33:10–11: "Thus saith the Lord: Yet again there shall be heard in this place . . . the voice of joy and the voice of gladness, the voice of the bridegroom and the voice of the bride."

The next level reads: *Yevorakh ha-bayit ha-zeh mipi navi ve-gam hozeh* ("May this house be blessed in accordance with the words of the prophet and the seer"). I was unable to determine the source of this phrase.

The next level states: *Ki malakhayv yezavch lakh Lishmarkha bekhal deralheykha* ("For He will give His angels charge over you, to guard you in all your ways").

This verse, Psalm 91:11, is recited in the home after the singing of *Shalom Aleikhem* on Friday evening. Psalm 91 is recited during the *Pesukei de-Zimra*, the introductory hymns and psalms on Sabbaths and Festivals and also after the Saturday evening service before the Havdalah ceremony.

On the level below is: *Or zarua la-zadik* ("Light will shine for the righteous"). This verse, Psalm 97:11, is recited as part of the Kabbalat Shabbat service on Friday evening. Some congregations chant it seven times on Yom Kippur, the Day of Atonement, before the recitation of *Kol Nidre*.

At the bottom of the Eternal Light is: *Adonai or li* ("[Though I sit in darkness], the Lord is a light unto me"). This is from Micah 7:8.

DIGNITARY SEATS

We deliberately demoted the dignitary seats on the bimah from their usual prominence. While searching archaeological records for general synagogue ideas, I uncovered reports of a "Seat of Moses." [5] I found that ancient congregations sat either on mats on the floor or on the stone benches that are still found along the side walls of many of the ancient synagogues. The elders sat with their faces to the people and their backs to the Holy (i.e., to Jerusalem). [6] The Seat of Moses was evidently for the most distinguished among the elders, as has been illustrated by the stone chair found near the south wall of the synagogue of Hamath-by-Tiberias [7] and in the synagogue at Khorazin. [8]

The Seat of Moses was a familiar physical object, not an abstraction. A Palestinian scholar of the fourth century C.E., Rabbi Ahai, facilitated the understanding of the biblical description of Solomon's throne ("and the top of the throne was round behind" [I Kings 10:19]) for his auditors by the simple explanation, "like the Seat of Moses." [9]

At Khorazin, the following inscription was engraved on the front of the Seat of Moses:

> Remembered be for good, Judan bar Ishmael, who made this synagogue and its staircase. As his reward may he have a share with the righteous.

Seat of Moses at Khorazin

[5] The earliest mention of this feature of ancient synagogues is found in the New Testament: "in the Seat of Moses" (Matt. 23:2).

[6] Tosefta, Megillah 4:21.

[7] Hamath-by-Tiberias is the site of a town that was called Hammath (from the Hebrew word *ham*, meaning "hot") in biblical times. The hot springs in this area, known for their curative powers, were supposedly created in the time of Solomon. Tiberias, the two-thousand-year-old capital of the Galilee, is situated on the western side of Lake Tiberias, also known as Lake Kinneret.

[8] Khorazin (also called Korazin and Chorazin) was a town before the second century, on the northern shore of Lake Tiberias. The remains of a synagogue of the third or fourth century C.E. were found here. In the New Testament (Matt. 11:21), it is said that Jesus preached to the people of this town. Rejected by them, he rebuked them, saying: "Woe unto thee, Chorazin." The city withered and died about five centuries later.

In fact, the site was not inhabited again until 1961, when Moshav Almagor was founded here and excavations began in the town area.

The synagogue, probably dating from the third century C.E., and destroyed in the fourth century C.E., was excavated in 1905 and 1926. A stone chair found inside is believed to be a Seat of Moses like the one mentioned in the Gospel of Matthew.

[9] *Pesikta de-Rav Kahana*, S. Buber, ed. (Lyck, Germany, 1868), p. 12.

There are those who identify this Judan bar Ishmael with Judan bar Ishmael the scribe, a person of the third century c.e. who is mentioned in the rabbinic sources.

A similar Seat of Moses was also reported in a synagogue in Kai-Feng-Fu, China, in 1704.

However, it has been argued by the noted scholar Cecil Roth [10] that the Seat of Moses "was in origin, not a ceremonial seat, but a stand in the form of a chair, in which the Scroll of the Torah was placed"; hence to "sit in the Seat of Moses," as Jesus states (Matt. 23:2), was a symbol of intellectual arrogance.[11] The Seat of Moses continued to have this function in the Jewish community of Rome and among the Jews of China. In the early Palestinian synagogues, the original purpose of the Seat of Moses was superseded and it became a mere symbol. Eventually the seat's original function was forgotten, and it came to be regarded as the vacant seat reserved for the Prophet Elijah, which he was supposed to occupy during circumcision ceremonies. Thus, in due course, the Seat of Moses became the Chair of Elijah. As Roth concludes, the seat, during rabbinic times, "was not intended for actual use."

Roth's thesis is rejected by I. Renov, who maintains that archaeological evidence, together with the Jewish and Christian literary sources, supports the hypothesis that the Seat of Moses "was a symbol of Jewish legal authority conferred upon leaders of Jewish law."[12] Possession of such authority was reflected in the institution of special seats for the leaders in a conspicuous place at the head of the congregation in the synagogue.

Beth El has copied the shape of the Khorazin seat for its dignitary seats, for the benches on the side of the bimah, and for the resting place for the Torahs.

For the comfort of officiants and other dignitaries, the hard stone seats have been upholstered by P. Nathan, Inc., of New York, in a specially designed gold velour fabric.

[10] Cecil Roth (1899–1970) graduated from Oxford and was for twenty-six years reader in the postbiblical studies there. He settled in Israel in 1964 and from 1965 until his death was editor-in-chief of the *Encyclopaedia Judaica* as well as a visiting professor of history at Queens College in New York.

He wrote profusely on Jewish history. Among his books are *A History of the Jews in Venice, A History of the Marranos, A Short History of the Jewish People, The Magnificent Rothschilds, A History of the Jews in England, A History of the Jews of Italy,* and *The Dead Sea Scrolls: A New Historical Approach.*

[11] More information may be found in the Hebrew periodical *Tarbiz* I-A: 145 ff.; Cecil Roth, "The Chair of Moses and Its Survivals," *Palestine Exploration Quarterly* 81 (1949): 100–111; and I. Renov, "The Seat of Moses."

[12] I. Renov discussed this in a paper presented at the annual meeting of the Society of Biblical Literature on December 27, 1950 (abstract in *Journal of Biblical Literature* 70 (1951): vi).

Seat of Moses at Kai-Feng-Fu

Thus, we have gone back two thousand years to place the rabbis and other officials on a level closer to the congregants.

LECTERNS

The rabbi's lectern, the reader's desk, the wedding ceremonial stand, and the menorah all have a bronze decorative design copied from the remains of a synagogue discovered on February 25, 1957, in the fields of Kibbutz Nirim, on the site of ancient Ma'on, or Menois.[13] The mosaic pavements of the ancient synagogue have a border of interlacing flowers pointing alternately outward and inward. Each of the flowers has a bell of three-graded shades of alternating blue and red, the deepest tone at the bottom and the lighter tones above it, with white petal endings and the whole on a black background. The border is flanked by two strips of black crow steps on a white background with outer white frames. This pattern occurs in many other synagogues, among them the fifth-century synagogue at Capernaum, the synagogue at Et-Tabgha, the synagogue of Na'aran, in sixth-century pavements at Beit Jimal, in the pavement at Nissana, in the fifth-century pavement at Antioch, and at Tebessa.

On the floor of the synagogue at Nirim, which is probably two thousand years old, there is an Aramaic inscription that reads:

> Remember for good the whole congregation.
> Remember those who have contributed this mosaic.
> And furthermore remember Daisin and Thoma and Judah.

As a further tie to our ancient Judaic tradition, we have picked up the mosaic border of the Nirim synagogue and used it for the metal decorating strip on our lecterns, reader's desk, ceremonial stand, and menorah.

Acacia wood is mentioned in the Bible as having been used for the original Ark of the Covenant.[14] Thus, the pulpit furniture in Beth El is made of wood similar to acacia. It was designed by R. Neill Gardner of Edgar Tafel's office and made by Warner Lane Interiors of Irvington, New Jersey.

[13] Nirim is in the Besor region of the Negev, northwest of Beersheba. Information about the remains found in this ancient synagogue was published in *Bulletin* III of the department of archaeology of the Hebrew University (1960).
[14] "And they shall make an ark of acacia wood" (Ex. 25:10).

Ma'on mosaic pavement

Above the pulpit of Beth El's sanctuary, situated over the area where the *huppah*, or traditional marriage canopy, is erected for wedding ceremonies, there is a transparent plastic dome.[15] The bride and groom stand under the view of the open sky as they join their lives together in the bonds of Jewish marriage.

The ceiling of the sanctuary is unadorned except at the joining of the walls, where there is a repetitive design of an ancient menorah, made of rolled zinc and painted in gold. Although a rolled ceiling decoration was very common in the nineteenth century, the builders could not locate a supplier for our architect-designed decoration. After much searching I found Miller and Doing of Brooklyn, the only existing manufacturer of rolled ceiling decorations in the New York metropolitan area.

EASTERN WALL

The cut-stone facing of the sanctuary's eastern wall, behind the ark, was developed from a suggestion by our rabbi, Dr. David I. Golovensky. It is a representation of the Western Wall in Jerusalem (actually the surviving outer courtyard wall of the Second Temple compound built by Herod). Our wall is a close reproduction of the sizes, shape, and colors of the Western Wall, even to the narrowest stones in the upper portion, which were placed on the original wall between the twelfth and fifteenth centuries, during the Mameluke period.

Some of our stone, the coping on the dignitary section, was quarried in the same area in Israel where it is thought that stone might have been cut for King Solomon's Temple. I traveled to Israel and visited the quarry when I was notified that work would commence on our stone. I approved the stone at the quarry near Jerusalem and again at the Lime and Stone Production Company in Haifa before it was shipped to New Rochelle.

Between the ark and the wall is a choir loft and an organ for weddings.

[15] The custom of erecting a huppah developed in the Middle Ages, and from this came the idea of holding the actual wedding ceremony outdoors, under the open sky. The huppah itself is said to be symbolic of the home that the new couple establishes in the community of the Jewish people. Rabbi Moses Isserles, the great sixteenth-century Polish authority, explains that weddings were performed outdoors as a sign of the promise that the newlyweds' children will be as numerous as "the stars of the heavens"—"Thus like the stars shall your children be" (Gen. 15:5).

You shall make a lampstand of pure gold: . . . note well and follow the pattern . . . shown you on the mountain.[16]

Beth El's menorah is one of the first menorahs to be carefully modeled on the menorah of the Second Temple, utilizing all of its details, including the three-legged base. Although a copy of an object two thousand years old, it is contemporary in feeling, and I believe it is a most beautiful adornment to our sanctuary.

I first learned about this menorah through an article in the *London Jewish Chronicle* of December 12, 1969. It described an excavation in Jerusalem led by Professor Nahman Avigad, head of the department of archaeology at the Hebrew University, with members of the Israel Department of Antiquities and Museums and Israel Exploration Society.

They had just uncovered probably the most authentic version of the original menorah in the Jewish portion of the Old City, just three hundred yards west of the Temple Mount. The site had been leveled, and excavations had revealed nine levels of building operations, apparently belonging to six different periods of history.

I was very excited about this find because we had examined and rejected dozens of artists' presentations for our menorah. I always had the biblical description of the Temple menorah in my mind, and here it was, an artistic rendering by a witness of the times.

Correspondence was conducted with Professor Avigad. Sketches of the menorah were prepared by R. Neill Gardner, and the menorah was ultimately fabricated by Warner Lane Interiors.

The gripping story of this rare archaeological find is recounted in the *Israel Exploration Journal*.[17] In digging down through strata dating from the Crusader and Mameluke periods, the excavators reached the Herodian period.[18] You can imagine the excitement when they lifted away the debris and came across the remains of an actual apartment with fragments of painted plaster. Here is an excerpt from Nahman Avigad's report:

Of particular interest are two fragments of unpainted plaster, found among the fresco fragments. These are incised with a seven branched candelabrum (menorah) of which the three left-hand branches are now missing. The height of the menorah is 20 cm, and its restored

*Two-thousand year old rendering
of Temple menorah*

[16] Ex. 25:31–40.
[17] Vol. 20, nos. 1–2 (1970).
[18] Crusader period: 1099–1291; Mameluke period: 1250–1516; Herodian: 37 B.C.E.–70 C.E.

width is 12.5 cm. Characteristic are the triangular base, the short stem and the tall branches which are proportionally higher than in any other ancient representation of the menorah.

All parts of the menorah are ornamented with what seems to be a stylized astragal pattern. The peculiar base requires further study: tentatively, one is inclined to interpret it as a tripod resting on a ring at the bottom, comparable with certain much earlier bronze lamp-stands found at Megiddo.[19]

Representations of seven-branched candelabra dating from before the destruction of the Second Temple are very rare. One such representation is known on the coins of Antigonus, the last of the Hasmonean Kings (40–37 B.C.). It is, of course, very small and schematic. Others, incised on the walls of Jason's Tomb in Jerusalem (first century B.C.–beginning of first century A.D.) are but simple sketches. The elaborate candelabrum of the Arch of Titus was carved in Rome shortly after the destruction of the Second Temple (70 A.D.).

The menorah found in the Jewish quarter of the old city—which, along with the frescoes, dates to the time of Herod—may therefore be regarded as the earliest detailed representation of the Temple candelabrum so far known. It was incised on the wall as a symbolic device at a time when the original object still served in its major ritual role in the Temple, only a short distance from the spot of our find.

The question arises, how faithful to the original is the representation? It is reasonable to suppose that the artist knew the original menorah by sight, and it is apparent that he attempted to reproduce it in detail. How far he succeeded, however, in giving a true image in his rather sketchy drawing, and how much should be credited to his artistic interpretation, is difficult to say. There does seem to be reason to believe that the general shape of the menorah here is closest to its prototype, as it is very similar in proportions to the representation on the coins of Antigonus. The menorah of the Arch of Titus is of similar proportions. This can hardly be accidental. In conclusion, it may be said that the representation of our menorah is a most valuable contribution towards a better knowledge of the original Temple candelabrum.

[19] Megiddo, one of the oldest cities in the world, is mentioned in ancient Egyptian writings from the time of Thutmose III. Called "Way of the Sea" in the Bible and "Via Maris" in Roman times, Megiddo was a bulwark of defense of Solomon's kingdom and was fortified by him. Many historical battles were fought here. Christian tradition says that the last battle of human history will be fought at Megiddo, which in the New Testament is called Armageddon.

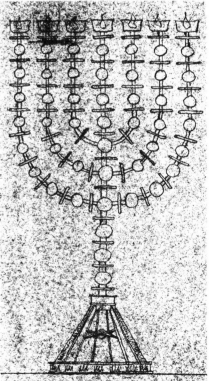

Original design of Beth El menorah, architect's rendering

A copy of the menorah on the Arch of Titus in Rome became the emblem of the State of Israel. A sculptured copy of that menorah stands in front of the Knesset Building in Jerusalem.

It is interesting to note that the menorah on the Arch of Titus and the one in front of the Knesset both have solid bases. Josephus, writing in the first century as an eyewitness to the removal of the menorah from the Temple by the Romans, stated that the construction of the menorah was changed from what it had been to a solid base.[20]

Maimonides[21] described the menorah as standing on three legs,[22] supporting Josephus' observations concerning the original menorah. This thesis was not completely proved until the excavation in December 1969 uncovered the menorah with three legs. The original plaster fragment with the painting of the menorah can be seen on display at the Israel Museum in Jerusalem.

Sometime after the menorah was installed in our synagogue, I met with Professor Avigad and showed him a picture of the menorah. To my chagrin he immediately asked, "Why did you change this detail?" He referred to the fact that our menorah has only one disk instead of two, as on the original. I had to explain that it was found necessary because of artistic balance. I regretted this lack of conformity. However, he was generally very pleased with our efforts. Shortly before Hanukkah of 1971, he wrote a letter to the children of our Hebrew school:

Dear Children:

Sometime ago when visiting in Jerusalem, Mr. Stanley I. Batkin, Honorary President of the Beth El Synagogue, showed me a picture of the Menorah which was recently installed in your Synagogue. The design was inspired by an ancient depiction of a Menorah found in the excavations carried out by the Hebrew University in the Jewish Quarter of the Old City of Jerusalem.

[20] Josephus Flavius, 38–100, originally known as Joseph ben Mattathias (Mattityahu) ha-Kohen, politician, soldier, and historian, was the Jewish commander in the Galilee during the war with the Romans. When his fortress was captured, he went over to the Roman side, took on a Roman name, accompanied Vespasian and Titus during the siege of Jerusalem, and then went to Rome. He wrote several books on Jewish history, including *The Jewish War*, which includes his account of the fall of Masada.

[21] Maimonides (Moses ben Maimon, also called Rambam, 1135–1204), was a philosopher and codifier. Born in Spain, he lived most of his life in Egypt as a court physician. He compiled a commentary on the Mishnah, the *Mishneh Torah* (which became a standard work of Jewish law and a major source for subsequent codes), and the *Guide for the Perplexed*.

[22] Menahot 3:7.

I think your Menorah is really magnificent and impressive, and I am sure that all of you like it and are proud of it. You certainly know the significance of the holy Menorah which served in the Temple of Jerusalem and became the unifying symbol of the Jewish people in the Diaspora and the emblem of the modern State of Israel. You may be interested to know the story of the discovery of our ancient Menorah in order to appreciate the full value of your new Menorah.

You see, at a time when the original Menorah was still standing in the Temple of Jerusalem, about 2,000 years ago, a citizen of Jerusalem residing in the Upper City just opposite the Temple Mount, decorated the wall of his room with a nicely executed drawing of the seven-branched candelabrum which he certainly knew personally from the Temple. Obviously, to him the Menorah meant not just a ritual object to use in the Temple, but also an expression of national and religious belonging and a symbol of eternal values—light, knowledge, eternal life.

Two thousand years later archaeologists in Jerusalem discovered the very same drawing of the Menorah in a layer of remains dating to the Herodian period. This Menorah became soon widely known in Jewish communities in the world over and your community chose it as a model for its new Menorah. Isn't it symbolic of the continuity of the history of our people?

The Hanukkah candles you are lighting are an expression of the very same values—the eternity of the Jewish spirit. I wish you a lightful Hanukkah.

Yours,
Nahman Avigad

Hebrew University, Jerusalem
Director of Excavations
in the Jewish Quarter
of Old Jerusalem

Beth El menorah

Most synagogues in the Western Hemisphere are adorned with two menorahs on their bimahs. I decided on one to avoid complete symmetry in the area and to concentrate on the beauty of this reproduction.

STARS OF DAVID

Directly above the bimah, in front of the two stained-glass windows, are two Stars of David. These were removed from the chandeliers of the old Beth El Synagogue on Union Avenue.

An additional two stars are in the ceiling of the reception room. These four stars are placed to delineate the exact dimensions of King Solomon's Temple, as mentioned in the Bible:

> And the house which King Solomon built for the Lord, the length thereof was threescore cubits, and the breadth thereof twenty cubits, and the height thereof thirty cubits.[23]

My original thoughts were to build our sanctuary to the exact size of King Solomon's Temple. However, our plot plan, the previous building, and the need to expand the sanctuary into other rooms for our High Holy Days services, prevented implementation of this plan. An interesting sidelight is the fact that the exact dimensions of King Solomon's Temple were duplicated in the construction of the Sistine Chapel in Rome.

STAINED-GLASS WINDOWS

> For he cast two pillars of brass, of eighteen cubits high apiece. . . . And he set up the pillars in the porch of the temple: and he set up the right pillar, and called the name thereof Jachin: and he set up the left pillar, and called the name thereof Boaz.[24]

The two windows on each side of the bimah were inspired by this description of the two columns, Joachim [25] and Boaz, that stood before the sanctuary built by King Solomon in Jerusalem. The narrow windows were chosen to reduce the possibility of glare or distraction to our worshipers. The windows are set in gray epoxy, a recent development in the art of stained glass. The epoxy seams, however, were specified a maximum of three-eighths of an inch thick to produce a higher proportion of glass on the surface. This is considerably less than the usual use of this cement as a bond for stained glass.

We decided to use the epoxy for the windows at the front of the building because they reached the ground level there and could be subject to vandalism. The epoxy is an almost indestructible form. The clerestory windows, high overhead in the rear, are leaded to give us more definitive designs.

The artist who designed the windows, Benoit Gilsoul, was born in Namur, Belgium, and is now a citizen of the United States, residing in

[23] I Kings 6:2.
[24] I Kings 7:15, 22.
[25] Jachin.

New York. He has won many awards throughout the world and has put on over fifty one-man shows in Europe and America. Included among these awards are the first prize at the Brussels World Fair in 1958. His works in the United States can be seen in the Interfaith Chapel at the United Nations; at Synagogue Beth Zion in Buffalo, New York; Synagogue Sons of Israel of Allentown, Pennsylvania; Temple Israel of Miami, Florida; and the Garden Jewish Center of Flushing, New York. Mr. Gilsoul's works are also found in many churches and public buildings.

Mr. Gilsoul was chosen for his deep biblical beliefs and knowledge, his rich, vibrant colors, and his rare artistic sweep.

The windows are an artistic re-creation of Joachim and Boaz. In designing these windows, the artist tried to show the telling and singing of the history of Israel with simple colored glass and transfigured light. Benoit Gilsoul described his work as singing the glory of God. He feels that each piece of glass is so assembled that it becomes a testimony and symbol of the living, active presence of the people of Israel in all the important events of the history of the world. The universal vocation of Israel is exalted. Israel is the connecting link between God and the nations.

These windows are not only a reminder of a journey in the past; they are the prayer of today and the hopes of tomorrow—the faith of a people and its confidence. When the colors are deep, they tell of the tragedies, miseries, pains, sorrows—and the menace of extermination. When the colors are loud, they sing the triumphs in the midst of difficulties, the great religious events, the culture, the intellectuality, the constant devotion to the enlightenment of humanity through the unending search for truth, justice, and peace.

The two columns are crowned by two dynamic and luminous lights—the moon and sun. The sun symbolizes the eternity of creation; the moon symbolizes the unity of the Jewish people and its mission, and the belief in the One God.

CLERESTORY WINDOWS

The rear of the Beth El sanctuary has fifteen magnificent clerestory windows, each picturing musical instruments of the Bible. Below this striking elevation is a list of the fifty-five prophets, according to Rashi.[26]

[26] Rashi (Rabbi Shelomo [Solomon] Yizhaki, 1040–1105), French Bible and Talmud scholar, studied in Germany, founded his own academy, and wrote a complete, definitive commentary on the Bible and Talmud. His commentary on the Pentateuch (*Humash*) was probably the first Hebrew book to be printed (1475).

Like the stained-glass windows, the clerestory windows were designed by Benoit Gilsoul, but they were created from my ideas in cooperation with our cantor, Lawrence Avery.

Mr. Gilsoul designed the windows to be 26 inches high by 61 feet wide. They are leaded stained glass, which is the traditional type of stained-glass artistry. We protected the windows from the elements by heavy plate glass on the exterior side. As the sun sets in the west, these brilliant glass windows create a colored banner of reflected light moving across our sanctuary seats and walls in the direction of the ark.

The musical instruments portrayed on the windows are clearly described in the Bible, and various representations of them have been made. The most recent, appearing on Israeli stamps, I supplied to Mr. Gilsoul as models for his work. The instruments represented (from left to right), together with the appropriate quotations from the Bible (italics added), are as follows:

Pipe
And his brother's name was Jubal; he was the father of all such as handle the harp and *pipe*. [Gen. 4:21]

Drum
And Miriam, the prophetess, the sister of Aaron, took a *timbrel* [drum] in her hand; all the women went out after her with *timbrels* and with dances. [Exod. 15:20]

Trumpet
With *trumpets* and the sound of the horn sound ye before the King, the Lord. [Ps. 98:6]

Also in the day of your gladness, and in your appointed seasons, and on your new moons, ye shall blow with the *trumpets* over your burnt-offerings, and over the sacrifices of your peace-offerings; and they shall be to you for a memorial before your God: I am the Lord your God. [Num. 10:10]

Tambourine
Praise Him with the *timbrel* and dance;
Praise Him with the stringed instruments and the pipe;
Praise Him with the loud-sounding cymbals;
Praise Him with the clanging cymbals. [Ps. 150:4–5]

Shofar
With trumpets and the sound of the *horn*,
Shout ye before the King, the Lord. [Ps. 98:6]

Blow the *shofar* [horn] at the new moon,
At the full moon for our feast-day. [Ps. 81:4]

Flute
And the harp and the lyre, the tambourine, the *flute* and the wine are at their feasts. [Isa. 5:12]

Ye shall have a song . . . and gladness of heart, as one goeth with a *flute* to come to the mountain of the Lord. [Isa. 30:29]

Psaltery
With an instrument of ten strings, and with the *psaltery*, with a solemn sound about the harp. [Ps. 98:4]

Cymbals
Praise Him with loud-sounding *cymbals* . . . and with clanging *cymbals*. [Ps. 150:5]

Harp
I will sing praises unto Thee with the *harp*. [Ps. 71:22]

Praise Him with the psaltery and *harp*. [Ps. 150:3]

And David and all the house of Israel played before the Lord with all manner of instruments made of cypress-wood, and with *harps*, and with psalteries, and with timbrels, and with sistra, and with cymbals. [II Sam. 6:5]

The flute, shofar, tambourine, trumpet, drum, and pipe are then repeated.

In Exodus 15:20, there is a reference to Miriam playing the drum (timbrel) after the song of Moses. Today, in Israel, one of the most popular instruments, used in dancing and singing both folk and popular music, is called the *tof miriam*, the "Miriam drum." It is usually made of clay or metal with a skin stretched across one end. It is played with the fingers, palms, or fists.

PROPHETS

Beneath the clerestory stained-glass windows are listed the names of the forty-eight prophets and seven prophetesses, as compiled by Rashi. There are various other lists of prophets, but for us the one by Rashi seemed most acceptable.

Abraham	Isaac	Moses	Aaron	Joshua
Jacob	Phinehas	Elkanah	Eli	Samuel
Gad	Nathan	David	Ahijah	Solomon
Iddo	Shemaiah	Elijah	Michaiah	Obadiah
Hanai	Jehu	Azariah	Ezekiel the Levite	Eleazar
Elisha	Jonah	Hosea	Amos	Amoz
Oded	Isaiah	Micah	Joel	Nahum
Uriah	Habbakuk	Zaphaniah	Jeremiah	Ezekiel the priest
Neriah	Baruch	Seraiah	Mahseiah	Haggai
Zechariah	Malachi	Mordecai	Sarah	Miriam
Deborah	Hannah	Abigail	Huldah	Esther

HOLIDAY MURALS

Arise, and go down to the potter's house.[27]

At its earliest meetings, the building committee resolved that the new building and its interior decorations should be expressive not only of our great Judaic heritage but of the strong bonds of tradition, culture, and brotherhood which bind the Jews of America to the Jews of Israel.

Where appropriate, Israeli artists were to be commissioned to execute representative works in a variety of media. Mr. Tafel, Beth El's architect, accepted the challenge of the building committee and journeyed to Israel to become steeped in the land and its people, the culture, customs, and attitudes.

I provided Mr. Tafel with a list of some thirty to fifty prominent Israeli artists—among them Gdula Ogen.

Gdula Ogen was born in Jerusalem. Her parents and grandparents, of Russian and Polish origin, had lived there for many years. She attended the Hebrew University from 1947 to 1949 and studied under Mordecai Ardon at the Bezalel School of Art from 1950 to 1952. She then trained with Hedvig Grossman of Bauhaus fame from 1953 to 1955. In 1955 Mrs. Ogen opened her own workshop in Jerusalem. In 1961 she received an award at the Exhibition of Mediterranean Ceramics in Stuttgart, Germany. Since 1962 she has held the post of chairperson of the department of ceramics at the Bezalel School.

Among the symposia in which she has participated are the International Seminar for Architectural Ceramics at Ein Hod in 1966 and the Architectural Ceramics Symposium in Austria in 1974.

Her commissions have come from the Hebrew University, Jerusalem

Gdula Ogen

[27] Jer. 18:2.

(1963); Museum Haaretz, Tel Aviv (1965); Zikhron Ya'akov (1968); the Weizmann Institute, Rehovot (1969); Bar-Ilan University, Ramat Gan (1972); and Bank Leumi, Jerusalem (1973).

Mrs. Ogen has had one-woman exhibitions at the Artists' House in Jerusalem in 1956 and 1975; at Maskit Shesh in Tel Aviv in 1967; and at the Museum Haaretz, Tel Aviv, in 1974.

She also exhibited at the International Exhibition at Brussels in 1958; as part of "Forms of Israel," a traveling exhibition in 1958; and at Expo '69 in Montreal.

When Mr. Tafel met Gdula Ogen and viewed her works, he was impressed immediately by their rough, primitive quality and their strength. Almost intuitively, he reported to me, he felt her capable of producing work of the towering proportions necessary to adorn the vast north and south walls of the proposed Beth El sanctuary.

Soon a voluminous correspondence, ultimately comprising several hundred letters, and typical of most of our art projects, started to cross the Atlantic. Some excerpts follow:

Jerusalem
June 29, 1968

Dear Mr. Batkin:

Thank you very much for the slides and your detailed letter of the second of May which gave me a better idea of the Sanctuary. For the murals I am now thinking of a repetitious element that will change size, rhythm and arrangement and will symbolize the links of tradition through the ages. It will at the same time be the unifying element for the ten murals and give it an architectural quality. . . .

Gdula

Jerusalem
November 11, 1968

Dear Mr. Batkin:

It is a long time since I heard from you. In the meantime I have been offered a stipend by UNESCO to study and visit in the Scandinavian Countries and England for three months for which I am leaving tomorrow. I did not want to face a situation that you will give me an order for a model and I will not be able to do it promptly, so during the last few weeks I prepared two models for two Festivals, the slides of which I am enclosing with this letter. They are Succot and Hannukah. . . .

Gdula

Tile work exhibited
at Museum Haaretz in Tel Aviv

New Rochelle, New York
January 10, 1969

Dear Gdula:

We were thrilled to receive your models and they had an enthusiastic reception here. While we understand the medium in which you are working does not lend itself easily to full detail, we would like the mural to fall within the middle of the following three types of art: realistic, recognizable impressionism and abstract. In other words, we want to be able to recognize clearly the object and the messages of each holiday. . . .

Stanley

The initial sketches by Mrs. Ogen were accepted and approved unanimously by our decorating committee. A contract was signed with her on March 13, 1969. Then followed:

Jerusalem
April 13, 1969

Dear Mr. Batkin:

Thank you for your letter. I will be looking forward to meeting you when you visit Israel. I understand perfectly that the panels must represent the symbols and atmosphere of each holiday. My task is therefore to find a way to express it in clay and to give it a three dimension quality. I feel it should at the same time be part of the building and not like a hung painting or a book illustration. I grew up in Jewish tradition, but still have investigated the details again about each holiday by reading Dr. Vahrman's book about the festivals and a new book about the ways of Jewish culture by Shlomo Ariel, prefaced by Chief Rabbi I. V. Unterman.

My next drawings in color will be very detailed and will show what each tile will contain and certainly all symbols and texts that will be used. As a three dimensional work, that should have an architectural quality, I believe it should not be very colorful. I intend to use several shades of brown, ochre, off whites and strong blues. My kiln produces a big variety of shades as I am firing the tiles in an open fire. I plan to use texts from the Torah and the prayers and wonder in what language should they be. . . .

Gdula

Shabbat   *Pesah*   ORIGINAL SKETCHES

Dear Mrs. Ogen:

It was a pleasure to receive your ten water color sketches and we are all thrilled with the effect and especially appreciate the considerable research that you have done into each holiday.

We are working on the submissions you have given to us and preparing the exact translations into English together with some change in quotations. While we are happy with the Biblical ones, we want to eliminate the others and add more pertinent quotations for each of the Holidays. The same is true of the symbols. You will hear from us regarding everything within a very short time.

The architect has had to change the dimensions slightly and we will also report to you on the status of that. . . .

Stanley

New Rochelle, New York
August 12, 1969

Dear Mrs. Ogen:

We are enclosing ten typewritten sheets for the phrases to be placed on each of the ten panels. Most of the phrases are in English but they are prefaced by one or two Hebrew words. One or two of the phrases are only in Hebrew such as the last item on the Sabbath and one or two are only in English such as the last item in Sukkot.

Wherever the Hebrew script appears use the one found in the Sefer Torah without the vowels. The dashes in English represent the fact that words have been omitted and these dashes should remain in your reproduction. Wherever the word God appears in Hebrew use the two yuds as on Rosh Hashanah 3.

On Shavuot put the Ten Commandments in Hebrew by using the first letter of each Commandment. This is explained on the sheet marked Shavuot.

On Rosh Hashanah items four and five are Hebrew words to be placed under two different Shofars.

On Hanukkah place item three on or near a dreidl. . . .

Stanley

Shavuot   *Rosh Hashanah*

LET THEM MAKE ME
A SANCTUARY

Yom Kippur

Jerusalem
August 29, 1969

Dear Mr. Batkin:

Thank you for your letter and check which arrived yesterday. I believe most symbols will be quite recognizable on the big panel. While I hope to manage with most symbols you suggested to add for some of the holidays, I find that in others, I will be unable to use some of the suggestions because of the medium I am working in. Also in some cases too many elements that have no space to flow into one another destroy the harmony and atmosphere of the work which I believe to be more important in this case than additional symbols or information. I am now starting with the clay models and you will be hearing about this soon. . . .

Gdula

New Rochelle, New York
September 16, 1969

Dear Mrs. Ogen:

We received your letter and you of course must do exactly as you say. Take the best out of our suggestions and reject the rest. . . .

Stanley

Jerusalem
October 4, 1969

Dear Mr. Tafel:

Thank you for your letter. I also enjoyed the visit of Mr. Batkin and his wife and was glad he accepted the models which I finished a few days before his arrival. It was nice to have a personal visit and be able to go into so many of the details which are continually coming up such as the size, application, plan details, etc. . . .

Gdula

Jerusalem
December 20, 1969

Dear Mr. Batkin:

Thank you for your letter. I hope to send the first of the three panels in March, the second set in June and the last four in

September or October. Thank you for informing me about the builders progress. . . .

Gdula

Jerusalem
February 19, 1970

Dear Mr. Batkin:

By now I have finished Pesah and started with Shavuot. The first and second panels are dry now for the firing. Everything goes well. I found no way of clarifying the items on the Pesah dishes in a realistic way so I did it by writing according to the Haggada as follows. . . .

Gdula

New York, New York
February 19, 1970

Dear Mrs. Ogen:

Work on the Synagogue is proceeding nicely. We are concerned about providing the necessary support for the tiles. Enclosed is sketch of our proposed method of anchorage. Please note that each of the three relieving angles will support five rows of tiles. Size of the angles is 1½″ x 2½″ x ³⁄₁₆″. Kindly advise us the exact size of the tiles, width, height, thickness and weight. . . .

Edgar Tafel

Jerusalem
March 14, 1970

Dear Mr. Tafel:

Thank you for your letter about the progress on the building. My work also progresses nicely and the three panels are now completed.

I believe there is no need for relieving angles. My tiles are deeply scratched on the back and will absorb the cement very well. The wall to the back of the tile should also be deeply scratched and an absorbent one. Both wall and tiles should be moistened. The tile should be soaked in water for about an hour and then taken out for a

Sukkot

while so that they are wet on the inside while drier on the outside to absorb the cement. The cement should be thick and fat, neither wet nor dry, made with ⅔ sea sand and some calcium to enrich it, etc. . . .

Gdula

Jerusalem
April 2, 1970

Dear Mr. Batkin:

My kiln is firing now and three more days of firing, three panels will be ready to be shipped over to you. The work is coming out fine and I hope you will be satisfied with it. . . .

Gdula

Jerusalem
April 12, 1970

Dear Mr. Batkin:

I received your letter and schedule and am looking forward to our meeting. I feel now it would be better to keep the panels here until after your visit so that we can discuss them. I am starting now with a new set of three panels and will do my best to have them ready for your visit. . . .

Gdula

New Rochelle, New York
June 25, 1970

Dear Gdula:

We were delighted to visit with you and thrilled with the result of your labors to date. The panels are simply magnificent and I am sure they will seem the same to others who will view them throughout the years. I am glad that we have arranged to have you be here to supervise the installation of the panels and make sure that everything is done properly. Would you please ship the six panels early in July and the remaining four in September. While the first six will go by boat, the last four can go by air if they are late. . . .

Stanley

Simhat Torah   *Hanukkah*   ORIGINAL SKETCHES

Dear Stanley:

Thanks for the color pictures you took on your visit here. By the time this letter reaches you the six panels will be arriving in New York. It is better not to let the shipments stay in the harbor. The box weighs about two tons and is well packed. I personally supervised the packing and checked them going on to the dock here. The only thing I did not do was to check the navigation license of the captain of the ship. I would prefer that you do not open the cases as the tiles are very brittle and should only be handled by knowledgeable people. My work proceeds on schedule. . . .

Gdula

Jerusalem
August 5, 1970

. . . [*via Western Union*]
Boat Eschgold *departed Haifa July 27th.*

Gdula

The shipment came in marked "ceramic tiles." We had to go through several appeals with the U.S. Customs inasmuch as ceramics are a taxable item whereas religious murals are not. We finally convinced the government of the religious nature of the art work.

Jerusalem
September 22, 1970

Dear Stanley:

I just received your letter with the list of English months and I certainly meant October and don't know why I mixed the names of the months. I am very moved by your invitation to stay in your home, while I am working on the installation.

It will be nice to have the party when the work is completed. We will all deserve a party and it should be for all of us. I am now writing a description of each of the panels for you.

Gdula

Purim   Yom Ha-Azma'ut

New Rochelle, New York
October 5, 1970

Dear Gdula:

Thanks for your letter and telegram. Cable us with the date of the plane shipment and give us your flight number as well. We look forward to your visit. . . .

Stanley

Jerusalem
October 26, 1970

Dear Stanley:

Your telephone call caught me unprepared and I could not hear you well. You must have received my letter in the meantime. To answer the questions on the telephone: I will arrive October 24th. To work efficiently I need the following: Two good workers and two helpers, a scaffold, a rich mixture of c/sand cement plus whiting (hydro calcium oxide). About 100 wooden wedges. Pieces of cotton (to keep the hands clean). Five—3/KG of powered iron oxide (the color of rust). Five containers—233 CM/deep by 33 Cm/wide—. These containers are to be filled with water to soak the tiles. Several hard hair plastic brushes (to brush the bits of cement from the tiles). A roll of thin rope (to keep lines straight all the way). . . .

Gdula

The first six panels arrived by ship; the last four were flown in by El Al. Mrs. Ogen soon followed to personally oversee the technical installation.

Working with a specially selected team of five tile setters, Mrs. Ogen then spent two weeks on the arduous and painstaking task of setting the tiles in place. At last the work was complete; the ten panels were installed in the Beth El sanctuary, there to inspire, to uplift, and to exalt the spirit of man.

The holiday murals may be viewed collectively as a ten-part work or individually as a portrayal of the essence and mood of the particular holiday depicted. The design of the panels is nonfigurative, and incorporated in each are appropriate excerpts from the Torah, Siddur,[28] or Mahzor.[29] The forms used in the panels are integrated closely with the scriptural texts.

[28] Daily prayerbook.
[29] Festival prayerbook.

Shabbat detail

II THE GREAT SANCTUARY *Bimah*

III THE GREAT SANCTUARY *Great Ark*

IV THE GREAT SANCTUARY *Eternal Light*

VI THE GREAT SANCTUARY *Menorah*

VII THE GREAT SANCTUARY *Menorah and Boaz Window*

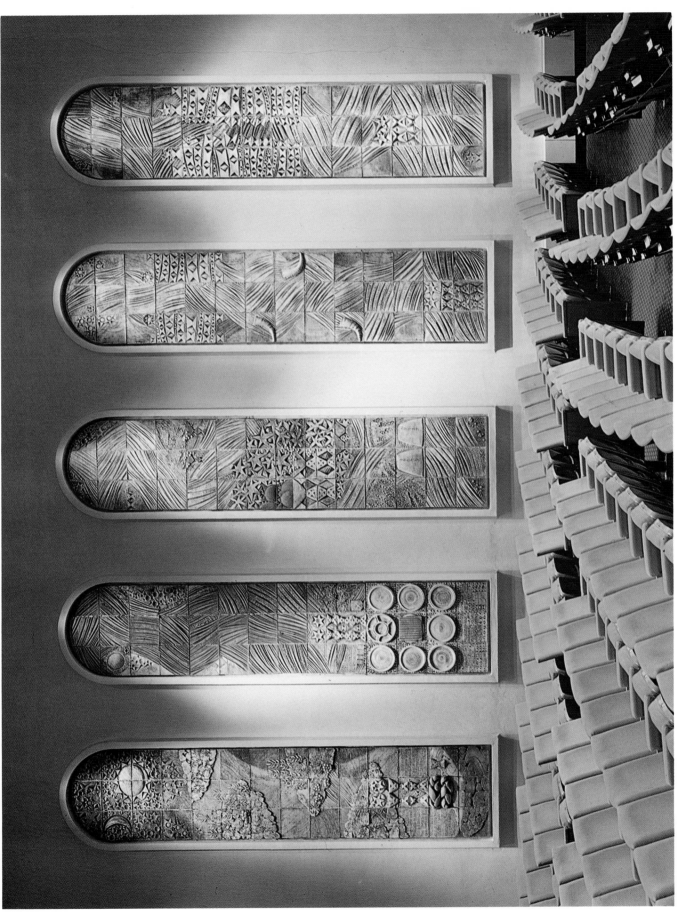

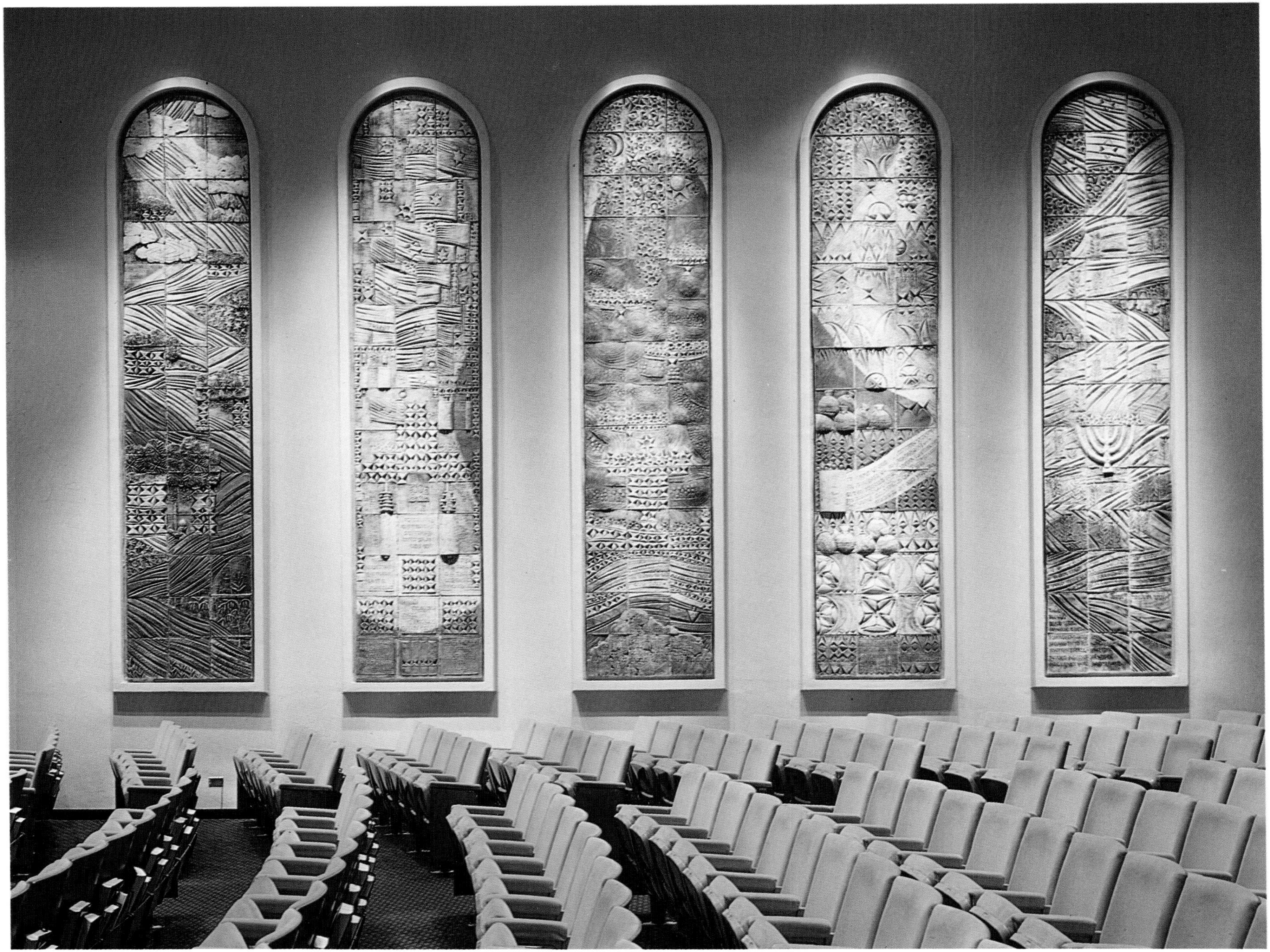

IX THE GREAT SANCTUARY *Holiday Murals*

WHY IS THIS NIGHT DIFFERENT FROM ALL OTHER NIGHTS

BEITZA ZRO'A KARPAS MAROR HAZERET HAROSE

XII   THE GREAT SANCTUARY   *Hanukkah and Purim Murals*

XIII   THE GREAT SANCTUARY   *Rosh Hashanah and Yom Kippur Murals*

12 The LORD spoke to Moses, saying: 2Speak to the Israelite people thus: When a woman at childbirth bears a male, she shall be unclean seven days; she shall be unclean as at the time of her menstrual infirmity. —3On the eighth day the flesh of his foreskin shall be circumcised.—4She shall remain in a state of blood purification for thirty-three days: she shall not touch any consecrated thing, nor enter the sanctuary until her period of purification is completed. 5If she bears a female, she shall be unclean two weeks as during her menstruation, and she shall remain in a state of blood purification for sixty-six days.

6On the completion of her period of purification, for either son or daughter, she shall bring to the priest, at the entrance of the Tent of Meeting, a lamb in its first year for a burnt offering, and a pigeon or a turtledove for a sin offering. 7He shall offer it before the LORD and make expiation on her behalf; she shall then be clean from her flow of blood. Such are the rituals concerning her who bears a child, male or female. 8If, however, her means do not suffice for a sheep, she shall take two turtledoves or two pigeons, one for a burnt offering and the other for a sin offering. The priest shall make expiation on her behalf, and she shall be clean.

13 The LORD spoke to Moses and Aaron, saying:

2When a person has on the skin of his body a swelling, a rash, or a discoloration, and it develops into a scaly affection on the skin of his body, it shall be reported to Aaron the priest or to one of his sons, the priests. 3The priest shall examine the affection on the skin of his body: if hair in the affected patch has turned white and the affection appears to be deeper than the skin of his body, it is a leprous affection; when the priest sees it, he shall pronounce him unclean. 4But if it is a white discoloration on the skin of his body which does not appear to be deeper than the skin and the hair in it has not turned white, the priest shall isolate the affected person for seven days. 5On the seventh day the priest shall examine him, and if the affection has remained unchanged in color and the disease has not spread in the skin, the priest shall isolate him for another seven days. 6On the seventh day the priest shall examine him again: if the affection has faded and has not spread on the skin, the priest shall pronounce him clean. It is a rash; he shall wash his clothes, and he shall be clean. 7But if the rash should spread on the skin after he has presented himself to the priest and been pronounced clean, he shall present himself again to the priest. 8And if the priest sees that the rash has spread on the skin, the priest shall pronounce him unclean; it is leprosy.

9When a person has a scaly affection, it shall be reported to the priest. 10If the priest finds on the skin a white swelling which has turned some hair white, with a patch of undiscolored flesh in the swelling, 11it is chronic leprosy on the skin of his body, and the priest shall pronounce him unclean; he need not isolate him, for he is unclean. 12If the eruption spreads out over the skin so that it covers all the skin of the affected person from head to foot, wherever the priest can see—13if the priest sees that the eruption has covered the whole body—he shall pronounce the affected person clean; he is clean, for he has turned all white.

14But as soon as undiscolored flesh appears in it, he shall be unclean; 15when the priest sees the undiscolored flesh, he shall pronounce him unclean. The undiscolored flesh is unclean; it is leprosy. 16But if the undiscolored flesh again turns white, he shall come to the priest, 17and the priest shall examine him: if the affection has turned white, the priest shall pronounce the affected person clean; he is clean.

18When an inflammation appears on the skin of one's body and it heals, 19and a white swelling or a white discoloration streaked with red develops where the inflammation was, he shall present himself to the priest. 20If the priest finds that it appears lower than the rest of the skin and that the hair in it has turned white, the priest shall pronounce him unclean; it is a leprous affection that has broken out in the inflammation. 21But if the priest finds that there is no white hair in it and it is not lower than the rest of the skin, and it is faded, the priest shall isolate him for seven days. 22If it should spread in the skin, the priest shall pronounce him unclean; it is an affection. 23But if the discoloration remains stationary, not having spread, it is the scar of the inflammation; the priest shall pronounce him clean.

24When the skin of one's body sustains a burn by fire, and the patch from the burn is a discoloration, either white streaked with red, or white, 25the priest shall examine it. If some hair has turned white in the discoloration, which itself appears to go deeper than the skin, it is leprosy that has broken out in the burn. The priest shall pronounce him unclean; it is a leprous affection. 26But if the priest finds that there is no white hair in the discoloration, and that it is not lower than the rest of the skin, and it is faded, the priest shall isolate him for seven days. 27On the seventh day the priest shall examine him: if it has spread in the skin, the priest shall pronounce him unclean; it is a leprous affection. 28But if the discoloration has remained stationary, not having spread on the skin, and it is faded, it is the swelling from the burn. The priest shall pronounce him clean, for it is the scar of the burn.

29If a man or a woman has an affection on the head or in the beard, 30the priest shall examine the affection. If it appears to go deeper than the skin and there is thin yellow hair in it, the priest shall pronounce him unclean; it is a scall, a scaly eruption in the hair or beard. 31But if the priest finds that the scall affection does not appear to go deeper than the skin, yet there is no black hair in it, the priest shall isolate the person with the scall affection for seven days. 32On the seventh day the priest shall examine the affection. If the scall has not spread and no yellow hair has appeared in it, and the scall does not appear to go deeper than the skin, 33the person with the scall shall shave himself, but without shaving the scall; the priest shall isolate him for another seven days. 34On the seventh day the priest shall examine the scall. If the scall has not spread on the skin, and does not appear to go deeper than the skin, the priest shall pronounce him clean; he shall wash his clothes, and he shall be clean. 35If, however, the scall should spread on the skin after he has been pronounced clean, 36the priest shall examine him. If the scall has spread on the skin, the priest need not look for yellow hair: he is unclean. 37But if the scall has remained unchanged in color, and black hair has

grown in it, the scall is healed; he is clean. The priest shall pronounce him clean.

38If a man or a woman has the skin of the body streaked with white discolorations, 39and the priest sees that the discolorations on the skin of the body are of a dull white, it is a tetter broken out on the skin; he is clean.

40If a man loses the hair of his head and becomes bald, he is clean. 41If he loses the hair on the front part of his head and becomes bald at the forehead, he is clean. 42But if a white affection streaked with red appears on the bald part in the front or at the back of the head, it is a scaly eruption that is spreading over the bald part in the front or at the back of the head. 43The priest shall examine him: if the swollen affection on the bald part in front or at the back of his head is white streaked with red, like the leprosy of body skin in appearance, 44the man is leprous; he is unclean. The priest shall pronounce him unclean; he has the affection on his head.

45As for the person with a leprous affection, his clothes shall be rent, his head shall be left bare, and he shall cover over his upper lip; and he shall call out, "Unclean! Unclean!" 46He shall be unclean as long as the disease is on him. Being unclean, he shall dwell apart; his dwelling shall be outside the camp.

47When an eruptive affection occurs in a cloth of wool or linen fabric, 48in the warp or in the woof of the linen or the wool, or in a skin or in anything made of skin; 49if the affection in the cloth or the skin, in the warp or in the woof, or in any article of skin, is streaky green or red, it is an eruptive affection. It shall be shown to the priest; 50and the priest, after examining the affection, shall isolate the affected article for seven days. 51On the seventh day he shall examine the affection: if the affection has spread in the cloth—whether in the warp or the woof, or in the skin, for whatever purpose the skin may be used—the affection is a malignant eruption; it is unclean. 52The cloth—whether warp or woof in wool or linen, or any article of skin—in which the affection is found, shall be burned, for it is a malignant eruption; it shall be consumed in fire. 53But if the priest sees that the affection in the cloth—whether in warp or in woof, or in any article of skin—has not spread, 54the priest shall order the affected article washed, and he shall isolate it for another seven days. 55And if, after the affected article has been washed, the priest sees that the affection has not changed color and that it has not spread, it is unclean. It shall be consumed in fire; it is a fret, whether on its inner side or on its outer side. 56But if the priest sees that the affected part, after it has been washed, is faded, he shall tear it out from the cloth or skin, whether in the warp or in the woof; 57and if it occurs again in the cloth—whether in warp or in woof—or in any article of skin, it is a wild growth; the affected article shall be consumed in fire. 58If, however, the affection disappears from the cloth—warp or woof—or from any article of skin that has been washed, it shall be washed again, and it shall be clean.

59This is the procedure for eruptive affections of cloth, woolen or linen, in warp or in woof, or of any article of skin, for pronouncing it clean or unclean.

XVI WEEKLY PORTION OF THE TORAH

In contemplating the panels collectively, as a unified whole, the viewer should be alert to the technique used by the artist to integrate the ten parts of her work. Firstly, there is a flow of color from each panel to its immediate neighbor, with the overall result that a gentle, wavelike color motion is achieved. Secondly, the artist has created a language of ceramic forms, repeated from panel to panel, so that all the panels speak in a common tongue.

The first form is a series of vertical, wavelike, upward-flowing lines. These lines create the feeling of a path or passage. Thus, in Yom Kippur and Rosh Hashanah, they are representative of prayer rising above and passing through the Gates of Heaven. In Yom Ha-Azma'ut, they are the way to independence. In Pesah, they symbolize the migration from Egypt and, as well, the pillar of fire and smoke which led the way through the desert. The element of the flowing lines is most dominant in the holidays associated with the outdoors.

The second form is a triangular design created by separating the two triangles of the Star of David. This element is repeated, changed by size, rhythm, and arrangement, and symbolizes the links of tradition throughout the ages. Thus, the links of tradition are rearranged to symbolize menorahs, Torahs, Hanukkah lamps, and Shabbat candle-holders—and in Yom Kippur and Rosh Hashanah, the very Gates of Heaven. In Purim, the shapes are given a comic turn expressive of the joy of the holiday. The triangular forms are most dominant in the holidays associated with the indoors.

Lastly, the panels achieve unity in that they are in quiet harmony with the other decorative aspects of the sanctuary. It is clear that the artist was at all times aware of the character of the room in which her panels would be housed.

The following descriptions may be noted when viewing the panels individually:

SHABBAT. The panel presents an atmosphere of tranquility and peace and an aura of fresh new existence. There is the feeling of the firstness of things.

At the base of the panel we see:

The heaven and earth were finished in all their array. On the seventh day God finished the work—and rested. God blessed the seventh day.[30]

We see the new lands with young plants and the first vines heavy with grape:

[30] Gen. 2:1–3.

Shabbat

Remember the Sabbath day and keep it holy.[31]

Above the earth but close to it is the Sabbath bread, hallot. Then we see the Sabbath candles, the Kiddush cup, the familiar Hineh mah Tov:

Behold how good and pleasant it is when brethren dwell together in unity.[32]

The single error by the artist was her spelling "bretheren."

The panel also has the greeting, *Shabbat Shalom*. Above in the heavens are the stars, the moon, and the sun.

Pesah

PESAH. At the base of the panel, the table is set for the traditional Seder: matzot as the central dish, the plate with the six portions of the Seder service, four cups of wine with a large cup for Eliyahu ha-Navi.

A sheaf of barley reminds us of the coming harvest.

In the upper panel, there is a column of fire leading the people from slavery to freedom. The moon is full. Next to the column of fire, the text reads:

I am the Lord your God who brought you forth from the land of Egypt, out of the house of bondage.[33]

Next to the Seder table, the text reads:

We were slaves in Egypt and God freed us. Had not God redeemed our fathers, . . . we, our children, and our children's children would still be slaves in Egypt.[34]

In addition there is the familiar Mah Nishtannah—

Why is this night different from all other nights? [35]

Shavuot

SHAVUOT. The rising lines again call to mind the exodus from Egypt. Here they also show the path by which the people bring

the choice first fruits of your land . . . to the house of the Lord.

The path passes through fields of wheat and corn, and on both sides, along the path, are arrayed the seven fruits. We see grapes, figs, pome-

[31] Ex. 20:8.
[32] Ps. 133:1.
[33] Ex. 20:2.
[34] Passover Haggadah.
[35] Ibid.

granates, olives, dates, wheat, and barley. In the center are depicted the *luhot ha-berit*, commemorating the gift of the Torah and the Ten Commandments, the greatest contribution of Judaism to the world.

Below are two familiar Shavuot quotations:

> You shall rejoice before God with your son, daughter, stranger, fatherless, and the widow in your midst.[36]

and

> Ve-zot ha-Torah—this is the Torah Moses placed before the children of Israel.[37]

ROSH HASHANAH. The shofars blast, and their song, mingled with the prayers of the people, rises up through the gates of Heaven.

> May the prayers of our lips find favor, exalted God, Who understands the voice of the shofar.[38]

Note the streaming lines both here and on Yom Kippur, symbolizing the prayers on their way up and into Heaven. The quotations read:

> On this day the world was called into being—all stand
> in judgment before You—
> be merciful unto us, O God of mercy.[39]

> Trust in the Lord. Be strong and let your heart take courage.[40]

Notice the two shofars with the wording in Hebrew—*Le-hayyim tovim* and *Le-shanah tovah tikkatevu*.[41]

Rosh Hashanah

YOM KIPPUR. "The day is waning," and the gates of Heaven are nearer and larger. They are closing. Three stars in the sky indicate the end of day. The people cry out:

> For the sin we committed before you under duress or willingly . . .
> by hardening our hearts . . . by the evil impulse . . .
> knowingly or innocently . . . Forgive us, O Lord.[42]

[36] Deut. 16:11.
[37] Deut. 4:44.
[38] Mahzor (High Holy Day liturgy).
[39] Ibid.
[40] Ps. 27:14.
[41] New Year's greetings.
[42] Mahzor.

Yom Kippur

Yom Kippur

Sukkot

Simhat Torah

Remember us unto life, O King, Who delights in life and seal us in the book of life, O God of life.[43]

Open for us the gate, O Lord, even as it swings closed, for lo, the day is waning.[44]

Repentence, prayer, and charity annul the severe decree.[45]

SUKKOT.   The mood of the panel is autumn. Again, the remainder of the exodus as the path winds and rises to heaven. Now the path is lined with booths, so that we may recall how our ancestors dwelt in the desert. In one booth are the lulav and etrog. Prayers for rain ascend the path to heaven. Atop the panel, heavy clouds give promise that the prayers will be answered.

At the foot of the panel, the aravah and hadasim plants grow alongside fresh water. The panel celebrates the last of the harvest and the ceremonial blessing of the waters.

Four familiar quotations may also be seen here.

You shall dwell in the booths seven days.[46]

Take the fruit of goodly trees—the etrog—branches of the palm trees—the lulav—boughs of leafy trees—hadasim—and willows of the brook—aravahs—and rejoice before the Lord.[47]

For the Lord will bless you—and all your undertakings.[48]

The season of joy.[49]

SIMHAT TORAH.   The panel portrays the three Torahs from which we read on this joyous day. The first Torah is open to the last paragraph of the Book of Deuteronomy. Here Moses blesses the Children of Israel just before his death.

Immediately we begin the reading anew in the second Torah with the familiar words of Genesis: "In the beginning God created the heaven and the earth." [50]

In the third Torah we read again:

She is a tree of life to them that lay hold upon her and happy is he that retaineth her.[51]

43 Ibid.
44 Ibid.
45 Ibid.
46 Lev. 23:42.
47 Lev. 23:40.
48 Deut. 16:15.
49 Festival Kiddush.
50 Gen. 1:1.
51 Prov. 3:18.

Reflecting our custom on this day, the upper panel is decorated with flags with Torah written on them, apples, and lights. Here we find four additional quotations pertaining to this holiday.

The Torah is a tree of life to them who uphold it.[52]

Rejoice with the Torah, for it is more dear than treasure, more precious than gems.[53]

O God, answer us on the day we call.[54]

And the familiar chant,

Next year in Jerusalem.[55]

HANUKKAH. The holiday of lights. The panel glows with the sparkle of the many Hanukkah lamps burning at night. We see the sun and the moon, the symbols of light. The dreidel is seen in the lower right corner. In the background are the towering hills of Judea with their terraces and villages, where

We kindle these lights in gratitude for the miracles, wonders and triumphs you wrought in times of old and in our day.[56]

In addition, we see the familiar chant, Ma'oz Zur Yeshuati.

O God, our saving stronghold, to praise You is a delight. Restore our house of prayer where we will offer You thanks.[57]

PURIM. Another joyous holiday. The festival table is set with jugs of wine and the traditional hamantaschen cakes and graggers. The panel depicts the *Megillah*, or Scroll of Esther, which tells the Purim story as it winds and turns on its way to heaven.
We read at the beginning of the scroll:

It came to pass in the days of Ahasuerus, who reigned from India to Ethiopia . . .[58]

And then the happy ending of the Purim story:

[52] Ibid.
[53] Prov. 3:15.
[54] Festival liturgy—prayerbook.
[55] End of Yom Kippur liturgy; also, closing of Passover Seder.
[56] Hanukkah liturgy—prayerbook.
[57] Ibid.
[58] Esther 1:1.

Hanukkah

Purim

The Jews had light and gladness, and joy and honour.[59]

The panel concludes with Maimonides' statement:

There can be no nobler joy than to gladden the hearts of the poor, the orphan, widow and stranger.[60]

YOM HA-AZMA'UT (Israel Independence Day). The path to independence is lined on the one side with newly placed trees and on the other with the graves of those who gave their lives to achieve freedom. The path starts low in half-light, and as it climbs higher into the full light, it turns into the national flags, with the Star of David on them and the stars of heaven about them.

In the center of the panel, amidst young trees, stands the menorah, symbol of the State of Israel and of Beth El Synagogue as well. The text looks toward a future of peace for all mankind as it quotes from Isaiah:

They shall beat their swords into plowshares,
their spears unto pruning-hooks:
Nation shall not lift sword against nation
nor learn war anymore.[61]

We also read from Amos:

I will plant them upon their soil, and they shall no more be plucked out of their land which I have given them, saith the Lord.[62]

In the lower right corner we see the tragic line, *Ani Ma'amin* (I believe),[63] sung by the millions as they perished in the Hitler scourge.

Yom Ha-Azma'ut

ADDITIONAL UNIQUE FEATURES OF THE SANCTUARY

SEATING. The seating consists of individual, theater-type seats, 374 in number, upholstered in gold nylon fabric with armrests and book racks. The seating was manufactured by American Seating Company,

[59] Esther 8:16.
[60] Maimonides, *Mishneh Torah*, Laws of Megillah 2:17.
[61] Is. 2:4.
[62] Amos 9:15.
[63] Maimonides' *Thirteen Principles of Faith*, daily prayerbook.

a leader in the field, and is identical to that in Philharmonic Hall at Lincoln Center.

REAR FOLDING WALL. The rear wall of the sanctuary is a folding wall with four individual pass doors. The wood is benge. The wall is broken by an interesting pattern of vertical amber glass panels, creating a heightened effect to the entrance and exit from the sanctuary. The hardware for the doors was especially designed for Beth El by R. Neill Gardner. The main sanctuary, sanctuary lobby, reception room, and ballroom are all connected through three folding walls. Each one, like the rear wall of the sanctuary described above, is decorated in conformance with the area it encloses. The congregation has an interesting and useful series of combination-sized areas available through the use of these folding walls. The main sanctuary can be enlarged in degrees, and during the High Holy Days it can encompass the four areas, seating eighteen hundred worshipers. The other areas can also be joined for enlarged uses.

Rear folding door during construction

MOTHERS' AND INFANTS' ROOM. Directly next to the main sanctuary is a room where mothers can leave their young children while attending services. The room has piped-in sound and a TV outlet from the sanctuary and has fully equipped facilities for this age group.

BRIDES' ROOM. A cheerful suite adjacent to the sanctuary, this room also has sound and TV available from the sanctuary.

WORSHIPERS' LOCKERS. Regular worshipers have individual drawers for their tallesim at the entrance to the main sanctuary.

RABBI'S SLOT. Next to the rabbi's seat on the bimah, there is an aperture where messages may unobtrusively be given to the rabbi from the choir loft area.

CHOIR LOFT. The rear of the bimah area is a choir loft.

OUTLETS FOR THE HARD OF HEARING. Several rows in the main sanctuary are provided with outlets for those who require amplification of sound to hear properly.

INTERCOM. There is an intercom system between the pulpits and the usher station.

ACOUSTICS. Due to the architectural and engineering planning of the main sanctuary, there is a rare acoustical effect, without echo. One can speak or sing, with or without amplification, with great clarity. Added to the natural conditions which our architect designed, a loudspeaker system was provided, with superior speakers. These speakers are spaced throughout the ceiling in square frames. The narrow vertical grills in the ceiling are used for air conditioning and heating.

LIGHTING. The lighting of the building was designed by a renowned lighting consultant, Jules G. Horton, and is a tribute to his extraordinary skill. The main areas have dimmer panels, enabling the lighting in different areas of the room to be changed to create various effects.

All the large circular openings in the ceiling contain downlights that have recessed gold-anodized cones. Directly in front of each of the ten murals is a set of three circular lights. These three lights, differing in intensity from each other, and each illuminating a different one-third of the mural, together provide an evenly lit mural that glows with a special quality.

There are smaller openings in the ceiling, running down both sides of the center aisle. When a bridal procession culminates with the appearance of the bride, most of the other lights in the sanctuary are dimmed and these two rows of lights brilliantly illuminate the progress of the bride to the bimah. On the floor of the center aisle are six sets of electrical boxes, hidden in the pews, used for electrified candelabra during a wedding procession. Spotlights for the ark are contained in the recessed ceiling above the ark, in the two vertical areas that are painted the color of the ceiling.

FLOOR COVERING. The entire sanctuary and bimah are carpeted in a Wilton three-tone blue, especially designed for Beth El by the A.B.C. Carpet Company of New York, and made by Langhorne Carpet, Bucks County, Pennsylvania. I prepared detailed specifications for the carpet after consulting federal and state specifications and comparing them to our traffic needs. We decided on three-frame 70 percent wool, 30 percent nylon, 10-wire, 252-pitch, 56-ounce face weight, 97.6-ounce-per-square-yard total weight, 3.75 pile. The basic design and color were developed in meetings with our architect and decorator.

DOOR PULLS. The door pulls were made to order in satin bronze from a design by R. Neill Gardner. Mr. Gardner and I toured New York clubs and hotels. I then drew a rough draft of my preferences, and he refined this into the final design. The door pulls and push plates were made by the Redstone Hardware Manufacturing Co., Inc., of Farmingdale, Long Island.

Door-pull sketch

THE SYNAGOGUE LOBBY

BLESSED WILL YOU BE IN YOUR COMING IN.
BLESSED WILL YOU BE IN YOUR GOING OUT.
                                    —*Deut. 28:6*

The synagogue lobby is a narrow, 17-foot-long hall used as an entrance-way from the main lobby to the great sanctuary. Its two long walls are folding doors made of magnificent benge wood. This hall can be used independently or to enlarge either the sanctuary on one side or the reception room on the other. The folding doors are 15 feet high, 64 feet long, and 2½ inches thick, and can be recessed into wall pockets. They were made by Fairhurst Industries, Farmingdale, New York.

WEEKLY PORTION OF THE TORAH

The weekly portion of the Torah, in the upper lobby of Beth El synagogue, is one of the most unique contributions to synagogue life in the English-speaking world.

For the week preceding each Saturday of the entire year, the English translation of the complete *Sidrah* (portion) of the Torah to be read that Sabbath is displayed for study and contemplation. The Torah, the written religious law for Jews throughout the world, is historically significant as the first great moral code for all mankind.

The panels are sixty-one in number, including the fifty-four regular portions of the Torah and seven double portions. The entire Torah—the first five books of the Old Testament—is divided into fifty-four weekly portions, each named after a key word in its first verse. These portions are read consecutively each week as part of the Sabbath morning services. The double portions are used to assure the completion of the Five Books of Moses within the one-year cycle. The panel is changed

Beth El Synagogue lobby,
sketch by architect

each Sunday morning; thus, in a period of twelve months, the complete Torah in English will have been viewed in its entirety.

Because the specific portion of the Torah read as part of the weekly Sabbath morning services each Saturday is recited in Hebrew, as tradition requires, not all the members of the congregation are able to understand its content and comprehend its message. It is also difficult to concentrate on the English translation in the Bibles provided to congregants while the Torah is being read aloud in Hebrew. However, thanks to the display in the upper lobby of the synagogue building, worshipers and visitors are able, at their convenience, to read the Torah chapter of the week in the latest English translation.

The unusual project of displaying the weekly English translations was germinated by my brother, Sanford Batkin, in 1967. Sanford, a Beth El trustee, is an active member of the synagogue's leadership. The idea was nurtured for seven years as many unforeseen obstacles were hurdled and many challenging problems were solved. The project was finally unveiled and dedicated on October 5, 1974.

The story of the implementation of the project is interesting in itself. After initial conferences in both New York and Philadelphia, the Jewish Publication Society of America granted us permission to use their printing positives—the first time in their history that they have given such copyright permission.

The text, published in 1962, is the most recent translation of the Torah by the Jewish Publication Society. This text supplanted the JPS translation of 1917, which is used in the Soncino (Hertz) Humash. The need for the new translation had been obvious for many years. Significant advances in archaeology and the recovery of ancient languages made the improved translation possible.

The Bible, being an eternal book, must be made intelligible to every generation. The language of the 1917 version, which imitated seventeenth-century English, seemed stilted. The new version, faithfully following the traditional (Masoretic) text but fluently utilizing present-day language, was prepared by a committee of distinguished scholars headed by Dr. Harry M. Orlinsky and including Dr. H. L. Ginsberg, Dr. Ephraim A. Speiser, and several distinguished rabbis.

Once permission was received from the Jewish Publication Society, we were able to move to the printing investigation. Here, various ideas were explored—printing on cloth, on parchment, projections, and so forth.

We decided upon clear plastic. Conferences were held with the General Electric Company, the Du Pont Company, and Rohm and Haas, each of which has products in this field. Several of these had various advantages, such as being nonscratch, but the nature of the nonscratch coatings made the printing process more difficult.

Finally, Rohm and Haas plexiglass was chosen—clear plexiglass sheets 48 by 32 by 3/16 inches. The printing was silk-screened in a special white ink to give the words of the Torah the effect of "floating in space."

The method of displaying the panels was carefully considered for several years. Sufficient importance had to be given to the Torah, commensurate with its primacy in Jewish life and the dignity with which it is usually enshrined. The final design, chosen after consultation with Roz and Morris Ratner, the donors, and many artists and designers, presents the panels in an altarlike setting, recessed behind a protective railing.

Beth El is probably the first synagogue anywhere to display the complete weekly portion of the Torah in such a permanent manner. Through an agreement with the Jewish Publication Society, Beth El can produce additional sets of the weekly portion of the Torah for sale to one congregation in each large metropolitan area.

By the time all the details had been worked out, the project was set back a full year by the ravages of circumstances: the executive director of the Jewish Publication Society and its officers had retired; the printer of the Torah, from whom we were to obtain the press positives, had gone bankrupt.

Negotiations were reopened; the Jewish Publication Society confirmed our agreement and arranged with their new printers to supply the necessary material.[1]

As Dr. David Golovensky, rabbi and spiritual leader of Beth El, said at the time of the dedication: "To my knowledge, Beth El is the only synagogue providing this valuable service to its worshipers and community."

The United Synagogue of America, at its biennial convention on November 16, 1975, presented Beth El with the Solomon Schechter Award in the "Worship and Ritual" category for the weekly portion of the Torah.

THE LIVING STAR OF DAVID

The Living Star of David in the lobby was created especially for Beth El Synagogue by the internationally famed Israeli artist Ya'akov Agam.

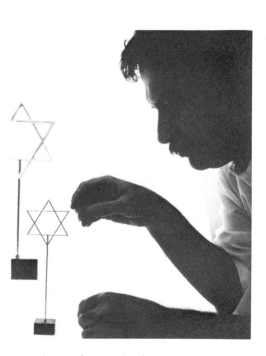

Agam demonstrating model of Living Star of David

[1] The printing positives were supplied by Haddon Craftsmen of Scranton, Pennsylvania. Jenssen Kurnos Designs made the proof sheets of the positive films and arranged them into the sixty-one Sidrah portions used to make the silk screens. The printing of the plexiglass was silk-screened by Design-A-Sign Company. The display was designed and made by Louis Maslow and Son. Models of the project were made by Martin Keating, Jr. The lighting to "float" the letters was designed by Jules Horton Studios. The intricate storage cabinet was designed and made by the Parson Woodworking Company. The electrical installation was by Nat Goldman and Son. Cantor Lawrence Avery divided the Torah to the various Sidrahs (portions) and approved the final layouts.

It is 9 feet high and 3 feet in diameter, and is made of stainless steel. A very subtle and detailed work of art, it was created, after much planning, to achieve a strong, soft, bold, spiritual, and living expression. The four shafts are mounted in a mechanical contrivance that makes them manipulable even at the light touch of a child's finger. The shafts can be turned continually to remake the Star of David by the interplay of the angled ends of the shafts.

In 1967, after I first discussed this project with Mr. Agam in Paris, he wrote:

> The Star of David has become, since the seventeenth century, a symbol related to Judaism. In the Living Star of David, I propose to attempt to create a constantly becoming and changing living symbol instead of a rigid and determined figure. The third and fourth dimensions which I will add to the symbol will express much better, in my view, the particularity of Jewish faith. The sculpture will also offer the viewer the possibility of active participation; one will be able to touch it, modify its inner structure and discover his own intimate relationship to it.

We agreed to his concept, and a year later, in 1968, the Star of David was on display in the grand foyer of the Petit-Palais in Paris prior to shipment to our synagogue.

Ya'akov Agam was born in 1928, the son of a rabbi of Rishon le-Zion. He studied at the Bezalel School of Art in Jerusalem until 1951, when he went to Paris. There, in 1953, he participated in the first exhibition totally composed of kinetic, movable, and transferable paintings.

Since then his works have been shown all over the world and occupy an honorable place in many excellent collections, including the personal collections of former presidents of France. In 1963 he received the first "prize for artistic research" at the biennial of Sao Paulo, Brazil.

Agam's work breaks with the established way of expressing reality. He demonstrates the principle of reality as a continuous becoming rather than a circumscribed statement. He has been deeply influenced by the Hebraic conception that reality cannot be expressed in a graven image, and that what is seen or observed consists of fragmented images which can never be grasped as a whole, even in very simple situations.

Thus, Agam pursues a course of research with the aim of creating an image that transcends the visible and cannot be seen completely at any one time. Such an image gives the viewer an understanding that he is receiving a succession of revelations beyond which lie unseen levels of reality.

Recently Agam has expressed these new conceptions in monumental architectural works, such as his *Jacob's Ladder*, which forms the ceiling

The Living Star of David demonstrated by Ya'akov Agam at the Petit Palais in Paris, 1968

at the National Convention Hall in Jerusalem. His *Double Meta-morphosis II* is in the Museum of Modern Art in New York. The *Forum Leverkusan* in Germany gained world attention. A transformable sculpture entitled *Three Times Three Interplay* was created for the Juilliard School at Lincoln Center in New York. Mr. Agam recently completed a room at the Elysée Palace in Paris for the president of France.

Dr. Haim Gamzu, the director of the Tel Aviv Museum, describes Mr. Agam as "the most famous of Israeli artists."

Moved by his friendship for my wife and me, Agam contributed to Beth El Synagogue the magnificent artist proof *Torah Mantle*. This work of art is inscribed "To Beth El Synagogue" and is signed by the artist. The rendering is in ninety-six individual colors, silk-screened by the leading exponent of this craft in Paris, under the personal supervision of Mr. Agam.

SUKKAH GARDEN

The glass doors to the Sukkah Garden bear the wording, "Blessed be your coming and your going." This inscription, taken from Deuteronomy 28:6, was found engraved on stone near an old synagogue in Spain, dating from the time of the eighth-century Moorish conquest of Spain.[2]

There is a similar inscription on the main entrance to the oldest synagogue in the Western Hemisphere, Congregation Mikve Israel-Emanuel on the island of Curaçao, established in 1654. I had wanted to use this wording somewhere in the building and the opportunity finally presented itself.

The lettering of the inscription, placed at eye level and then repeated at a lower height, provides conformance with local building codes, which require a bar or marking on glass doors to ensure that people will not walk accidentally into the door. The letters were carefully chosen for the dual purpose and were printed on clear pressure-sensitive acetate for application to the glass door. The effect is one of lettering floating in space. Here we answered a twentieth-century requirement with a biblical quotation.

The pattern here was similar to many other courses incorporating my thoughts in the building: first an idea, a location, a search for the medium and the artist, and then the implementation.

Jenssen Kurnos Designs provided the lettering. I searched long and hard to find a printer capable of making such a short run in a highly

Cong. Mikvé Israel-Emanuel of Curaçao 1654

---

[2] Benjamin Mazar and Moshe Davis, *The Illustrated History of the Jews* (New York: Harper and Row, 1963), p. 207.

specialized area of clear pressure-sensitive acetate. Litho-Etch Metal Name Plate Company, of Bronx, New York, was finally located for this purpose.

POOL OF THE LEVITES

My fact sheet for the proposed Pool of the Levites stated:

The Pool of the Levites is 6′ wide by 3′ 8″ outside dimensions. The mosaic lining on the interior of the pool will be 4′ 8″ wide, 3′ long and 1′ 6″ deep. It will have a decorative railing 5′ 4″ in the front and 3′ 4″ on either side. The height of the railing is 6″. It is hoped to copy an old mosaic Synagogue floor and also a decorative railing from the Laver of Solomon's Temple. The pool will contain fish native to Israel.

The Pool of the Levites in the lobby of Beth El Synagogue has two unique features: first, it is lined with a detailed mosaic copy of the floor of the sixth-century synagogue Bet Alfa in the Jezreel Valley; second, it has a bronze railing, faithfully reproducing a description of the laver in King Solomon's Temple.

This project came closer to reality when, during one of my search and study visits to Israel, I was attracted by the magnificent, well-preserved floor of the Bet Alfa synagogue. I immediately knew that my search for a mosaic floor was over. How to reproduce this floor was another matter. After several years of investigation, I heard about Kibbutz Eilon, on Israel's Lebanese border, where mosaic murals and other items are made from native stone.

Kibbutz Eilon was founded in 1938 as a "wall and tower" camp by prewar emigrants from Poland. These people were subsequently joined by others, who fought their way to Israel during World War II. Today the kibbutz sustains over six hundred people, and the mosaic operation is but one of its various enterprises.

Negotiations with Meir Davidson, the manager of the kibbutz workshop, and Mordecai Yoeli, the artist, were conducted in Tel Aviv, at the kibbutz itself, and across the Atlantic. After eighteen months an agreement was made. Sometime thereafter I found that a Beth El family, my dear friends Florence and Harold Drimmer, were related to Davidson and could have saved me the years of investigative effort.

The mosaic lining was designed by Mordecai Yoeli. Mr. Yoeli was born in Baronowicze, Eastern Poland, in 1916. He immigrated to Israel in 1939 and joined Kibbutz Eilon, then a pioneer settlement. The kibbutz gave him an opportunity to study at the Bezalel School of Art

Mordecai Yoeli

in Jerusalem. On his return, others joined in the work on mosaics, and today dozens of Eilon mosaics decorate various institutions and buildings in Israel and abroad, including synagogues, schools, and banks. The mosaic artisans use natural stones of various shades brought to the kibbutz from all over Israel, as far south as the Timna Mountains. They use an ingenious plastic material for holding the stones together instead of the customary cement used throughout the world.

The fine taste shown by the artists on the kibbutz in shaping the mosaics creates a bridge between the innovations of the present generation and Israel's rich heritage in the early development of mosaic works.

After a study of mosaics I determined that stones of three to five millimeters in size were necessary to achieve the clarity this mosaic required. The smallest stones the kibbutz had previously worked on were ten millimeters. They agreed, however, to execute our commission in the five-millimeter size to satisfy our needs.

The discovery of the Bet Alfa floor and the relation of the zodiac to Judaism is another interesting story. I received some information concerning these matters from the library of the Jewish Theological Seminary of America, the National Parks Authority of Israel, and Rabbi Edmund Winter, who studied the subject for me.

The Bet Alfa settlement is situated on the northern slope of the Gilboa Mountains, which form the southern boundary of the Jezreel Valley in the Galil section of Israel. At the end of December 1928, settlement members reported that in the course of digging a channel for conveying water to their fields, they had come upon the remnants of a building paved with mosaic. After it had been cleaned, there could be seen certain signs of the zodiac, and above them, Hebrew characters. Later excavations revealed the remains of a synagogue and a well-preserved mosaic pavement. It was from this pavement that the mosaic of Beth El Synagogue's Pool of the Levites was copied.

The original structure of the Bet Alfa synagogue consisted of an almost square forecourt, a narrow hall and rectangular prayer chamber, and the synagogue proper, with an apse in its southern wall, facing Jerusalem, which originally held the ark of the Law. Two colonnades divided the synagogue into nave and aisles. The women's galleries were above the aisles. From the fallen stones among the debris it was clear that the original roof had been gabled. In the center of the apse, beneath the ark, the archaeologists found a small pit covered by stone slabs. It had, no doubt, been used to safeguard the synagogue treasures, for it still contained a number of coins. Their dates—plus an inscription on the floor—confirmed the dating of the construction as sixth century.

The entire floor of the nave was covered by an elaborate mosaic, still virtually intact, divided into three panels and bordered on three sides by geometric designs and representations of animal and plant life.

*Floor mosaics
at Bet-Alfa Synagogue*

Preliminary sketch

Beth El mosaic

Below the fourth side is an inscription, set between a bull and a lion, recording that the floor was laid during the reign of the Emperor Justin. The ruler referred to could be either Justin I (518–27) or Justin II (565–78) and it is difficult to decide between these alternatives. The panel near the apse depicts the emblems of the Jewish ritual service. At the center is the ark, and on either side are a lion, a bird, and a seven-branched candelabrum. The large central panel presents the twelve signs of the zodiac, with the symbols of the months and their names in Hebrew and Aramaic. The lower panel is an illustration of the biblical story of Abraham's would-be sacrifice of Isaac, accompanied by explanatory verses in Hebrew from the Bible. Above the ram tied to a tree are the words "Behold the ram." The staying hand emerging from the heavens is captioned "Lay not" (thine hand upon the lad). The names Abraham and Isaac are inscribed above their heads.

Within the inner circle of the Bet Alfa mosaic is a symbolic picture of the sun riding in a chariot drawn by four galloping horses. This picture portrays the most important moment in the sun's daily circuit, as the sun rises out of the darkness of night.

This motif, the sun in the act of rising, is based on the traditional portrayal of Helios in Greek art. The nearest parallel to the Bet Alfa representation is a picture on a fifth-century B.C.E. vase, now in the British Museum.

In the literature of the period, we find an echo of this representation of the sun.

In the heart of the Sun are written three of the letters of the name [of God], and it is drawn along by eight angels. They which draw it by day are other than they which draw it by night; they which draw it by night are other than they which draw it by day. The Sun rides in a chariot and arises crowned like a bridegroom and he rejoices like a mighty man, as it is written, "as a bridegroom cometh forth out of his chamber." [3]

In the Beth El mosaic, within the inner circle is the breastplate of the high priest, containing twelve different colored stones which represent the twelve tribes of Israel.

In the outer circle are pictures of the twelve signs of the zodiac. The signs are separated by broad bands of guilloche, various geometrical patterns, and other decorations. The signs of the zodiac begin at the right of the Chariot of the Sun and go around in counterclockwise fashion.

In depicting Cancer, the fourth sign of the zodiac, the craftsman chose a local species of crab, *Potamion potamios*, which lives in the Jalud

[3] *Pirke de Rabbi Eliezer*, par. 6, edited by Samuel Loria (Warsaw, 1852).

XVII LIVING STAR OF DAVID

XVIII POOL OF THE LEVITES

XIX RAILING AT POOL OF LEVITES

XXIII LEVENSON CHAPEL *Wall of the Tribes*

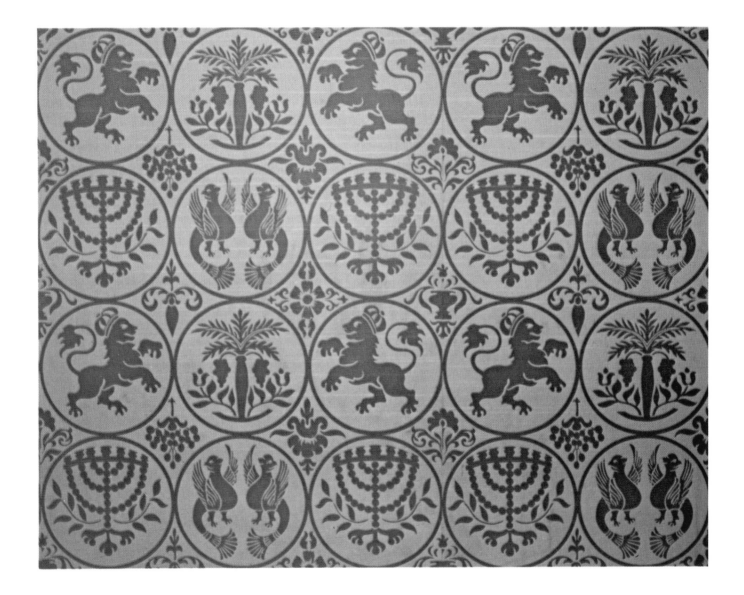

XXIV GOLDBERGER CHAPEL *Beth El Mahzor Wallpaper*

River of the Jezreel Valley. The crab is portrayed lying on its back, leaving its eyes invisible.

The style in which Virgo is portrayed is an unusual one for signs of the zodiac: a golden-haired woman with her hands in her lap sits on a throne; only the round top of the throne and two projections from its upholstered seat can be seen. This portrayal of a throne is the oldest example in the East.

As often in Roman art, so at Bet Alfa, the seasons are portrayed as winged cherubs, showing only the upper part of the bodies. They are distinguished from one another both by descriptive inscriptions and by the attributes peculiar to each season.[4]

THE TWELVE ZODIACAL SIGNS. The first mention in Jewish literature of the division of the zodiac into twelve constellations is found in a mystical work of the first century C.E. called *Sefer Yezirah*. A list of the zodiacal signs is given that corresponds to the twelve Hebrew months. According to another rabbinic statement, each sign of the zodiac corresponds to the standard of one of the twelve tribes. For all the correlations, refer to the following table.

TABLE OF CORRESPONDENCES

Zodiacal Sign	Hebrew Name	Standards of Tribe	Hebrew Month
Aries	Taleh	Judah	Nisan
Taurus	Shor	Issachar	Iyar
Gemini	Te'omim	Zebulun	Sivan
Cancer	Sartan	Reuben	Tammuz
Leo	Aryeh	Simeon	Av
Virgo	Betulah	Gad	Elul
Libra	Moznayim	Ephraim	Tishri
Scorpio	Akrav	Manasseh	Heshvan
Sagittarius	Kashat	Benjamin	Kislev
Capricorn	Gedi	Dan	Tevet
Aquarius	Deli	Asher	Shevat
Pisces	Dagim	Naphtali	Adar

According to the author of *Sefer Yezirah*, the signs also correspond to the following twelve central bodily organs: two hands, two feet, two

[4] Eleazer L. Sukenik, *The Ancient Synagogue of Beth Alpha* (Jerusalem: The University Press, 1932).

kidneys, gall bladder, intestines, liver, throat, stomach, and pancreas. This order harmonizes with that of the Assyrians, who also designated the zodiacal signs according to the organs of the body: head, neck, arms, breast, heart, bowels, kidneys, loins, thighs, knees, legs, and feet.

A later, more detailed division of the zodiac is to be found in this quotation from the Talmud:

> God said to Israel: "My daughter, twelve zodiacal constellations are in the firmament, each station of the Zodiac has thirty paths and each path has thirty legions of stars, have I not created all of these for your sake, yet you say: 'You have forsaken and forgotten me.'"[5]

SYMBOLISM. The basis of the symbolism of the zodiacal signs as recorded in Jewish literature can be traced to Assyrian mythology and influence. It found its way into Judaism during the Babylonian exile, when the Jews adopted Hebraized forms of the Assyrian names of the months and the constellations. However, our sages were not content with a simplistic understanding of the significance of the zodiac; instead they searched for a more profound and meaningful connection between the signs and their own experience.

For example, our rabbis tried to explain the origin of the names of the zodiacal signs by relating them to the destruction of the Temple:

> Another comment: "And there was woe when Zedekiah, the son of Josiah reigned as king."[6] Why was the Temple not destroyed in the first month of the year, or in the second month, or in the third, or in the fourth, why in the fifth? The fact is God wanted to destroy the Temple in the first month [Nisan, whose zodiacal sign is the lamb]. But the merit of Isaac stood forward to plead. "Master of the Universes, remember the sacrifice for which I let myself be tied up before Thee: I offered myself as a lamb for the sacrifice, instead of the sacrificial lamb." Then God wanted to destroy the Temple in the second month [Iyar, whose zodiacal sign is the bull]. But the merit of Abraham stood forward, as it said, "and Abraham ran into the herd and fetched a young bull."[7] So God wished to destroy the Temple in the third month [Sivan, whose zodiacal sign is twins]. But the merit of Jacob stood forward, as is said "and the boys [Jacob and Esau] grew."[8] Then God wanted to destroy the Temple in the fourth month [Tammuz, whose zodiacal sign is the crab]. But

[5] Berakhot 32b.
[6] Jer. 37:1.
[7] Gen. 18:7.
[8] Gen. 25:27.

the merit of Moses stood forward to plead: "the crab can draw its life only from the water, and my life was drawn from the water." When God was about to destroy the Temple in the fifth month [Av, whose zodiacal sign is the lion] there was no merit to assuage His wrath. So God said: It is fitting that Nebuchadnezzar come, he who is called lion,[9] to destroy the Temple which is described as "the lion of God"[10] and to smite Israel also termed "lion"[11] it is fitting that destruction come in the month whose zodiacal sign is the lion, because the children of Israel set aside the words of the lion, He of whom it is said "The lion hath roared, who will not fear?" in Amos 3:8.[12]

The hidden symbolism of the zodiac, for the Jew of the fourth to fifth century B.C.E., is revealed by the following two facts. The zodiac penetrated the Jewish world as an astrological, rather than an astronomical, device. Thus the zodiac could foretell the "end of days," the advent of the Messianic age, the restoration of the "Crown of Kingdom" to Israel. In Jewish sources the constellation Leo, which in pagan astrology represented the "house" of the sun—the big luminary, became the protector of Rome, descendant of Esau, "the big one." And the constellation Cancer, from which the lunar constellations were counted —the "house" of the moon, the small luminary, became the protector of Israel, descended from Jacob, the "small one." Thus by placing Cancer at the very top of the zodiacal circle in the direct view of the congregation facing the holy shrine, the designer conveyed the Jewish hope of throwing off the yoke of Rome (Byzantium) and capturing the "Crown of Kingdom."

ASTROLOGICAL USE OF THE ZODIAC. Throughout the ages, astrology has been a center of controversy among all mankind, even among Jews. Maimonides, basing himself on the biblical passage, "you shall not observe times,"[13] declared that belief in the influence of the stars on human events is "deserving of flagellation."[14] In a letter he denounced astrology as "a disease, not a science, a tree under the shadow of which all sorts of superstitions thrive, and which must be uprooted in order to give way to the tree of knowledge and the tree of life."[15]

[9] Jer. 4:7.

[10] Is. 29:1.

[11] Num. 23:24.

[12] *Pesikta Rabbati* 27, 28, translated and annotated by William G. Braude (New Haven: Yale University Press, 1968), p. 547.

[13] Lev. 19:26.

[14] Maimonides, *Mishneh Torah*, Hilkhot Avodat Kokhavim, 11:9.

[15] Isadore Twersky, ed., *A Maimonides Reader* (New York: Behrman House, 1972), p. 473.

Joseph Karo, the author of the *Shulhan Arukh*, concurs with Maimonides that one may not consult stargazers, but for a different reason. The stars should not be consulted because the Bible commands: "You shall be perfect with the Lord your God." [16] "Therefore, our sages warned man not to give thought to these things, but rather let him attach himself to the One who spoke and created the world, and He in His mercy will save His servant from many evils." [17] Judaism's goal of direct individual communion with God cannot be achieved through an intermediary.

Yet in the final analysis, halakhically, Karo takes a more moderate position than Maimonides, neither accepting nor disregarding astrology. Thus: marriages ought not be contracted on days of the moon's decline; new projects should not be started on the second or fourth day of the week. According to the *Shulhan Arukh*, to place confidence in the zodiac is forbidden; but to ignore its warnings is to be foolhardy.

RAILING AROUND THE POOL OF THE LEVITES. The railing around our Pool of the Levites was inspired by the ten movable lavers of King Solomon's Temple, described in I Kings 7:27–29 and II Chronicles 4:6. While these descriptions are very detailed, they present great difficulties because the meanings of a number of technical terms are not certain. A reconstruction based on the biblical descriptions, therefore, is highly conjectural. We do know, however, that the bronze stands were decorated with a whole collection of beasts, evidently symbolic bulls, lions, cherubim, and various vegetal or linear motifs (palm trees and scrolls).

From this information, and from studies made by André Parrot,[18] professor at the Louvre in Paris, and others, we have designed this reminder of the laver of King Solomon's Temple. The railing was made by Warner Lane Interiors.

[16] Deut. 18:13.
[17] *Beit Yosef, Yoreh De'ah*, p. 179.
[18] André Parrot, *Ninive et l'ancien Testament* (Neuchâtel: Delachaux & Niestlé, 1955).

THE CHAPELS AND REMEMBRANCES

OH LORD, I LOVE TO DWELL IN THY HOUSE
AND THE DWELLING PLACE OF THY GLORY.
—*Psalms 26:8*

THE LEVENSON CHAPEL

The Levenson Chapel is a light, charming room built in a closely responsive schematic layout simulating the Sephardic type of synagogue. It was especially built for our five-to-thirteen-year-old children, who hold regular Shabbat and holiday services. The chapel is also used by other groups for lectures, meetings, classes, and special religious services. It can seat between sixty and one hundred people, depending on age.

THE ARK. The ark features the stones of the twelve tribes, each five-eighths of an inch in size and mounted on a contemporary pewter plaque bearing the name of the tribe. These are arranged in four vertical rows, beginning on the left side of the ark.

First Row

Carnelian	Reuben
Topaz	Simeon
Smaragd	Levi

Second Row

Carbuncle	Judah
Sapphire	Dan
Emerald	Naphtali

Third Row

Jacinth	Gad

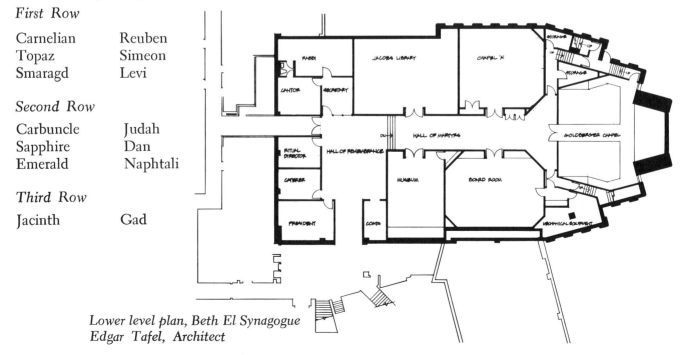

Lower level plan, Beth El Synagogue
Edgar Tafel, Architect

Agate   Asher
Amethyst   Issachar

Fourth Row

Beryl   Zebulun
Onyx   Joseph
Jasper   Benjamin

This arrangement follows the Aramaic translation of Jonathan, son of Uziel, who listed the tribes according to the order of birth of the sons of Jacob, beginning with the first-born.

There is, however, another arrangement. It follows the Jerusalemite Aramaic translation, and is based on the relationships of the mothers: six sons of Leah, two sons of Bilhah, two sons of Zilpah, two sons of Rachel.

First Row

Carnelian   Reuben
Topaz   Simeon
Smaragd   Levi

Second Row

Carbuncle   Judah
Sapphire   Issachar
Emerald   Zebulun

Third Row

Jacinth   Dan
Agate   Naphtali
Amethyst   Gad

Fourth Row

Beryl   Asher
Onyx   Joseph
Jasper   Benjamin

The ark in the Levenson Chapel was a contribution of Richard Maslow of Louis Maslow and Sons. Mr. Maslow, not a member of our community, was a contractor on portions of the building, and he was inspired to perform this generous voluntary act at that time.

THE PAROKHET. The *parokhet* (curtain) on the ark was personally designed and made by Hannelies Guggenheim in memory of her late husband, Jules. Mrs. Guggenheim describes her work:

> My aim throughout the creation of the Parokhet was to communicate the joy of Torah to our young congregants. I decided to offset the deep brown of the ark's wood with the blue and silver of the chapel's walls. After settling on the basic color combination, I travelled to several mills in New England to find the most suitable yarns. I spent many weeks at my small sample loom, trying to find a pattern which would be simple, rich in texture, yet not ornate.
>
> Bearing in mind the biblical prohibition of mixing animal with vegetable fibers, I came upon a mixture of linen, cotton, rayon, mylar and chenille. The pattern is set 20 threads to the inch, basically a twill weave, executed on an 80 harness Bergman loom. I used ten different types of yarn in the warp, and the weft combines three varieties of yarn, necessitating a delicate balance of three shuttles.
>
> Appliqued on the beige and silver background are blue, silver and white discs depicting variations of the theme of the Mogen David. The discs were created by adapting a technique of "wrapping" which dates back to the early 1700's, when sailors "wrapped" to wile away the long months of whaling boats at sea. Each thread must be placed at the precise spot to yield the desired pattern. I felt that these simple geometric forms would appeal to the children, while echoing the motifs found along the opposite wall in the chapel.

MURALS. The murals on the two front walls are a prominent artistic adornment of the chapel: on the right, the Wall of Coins; on the left, the Wall of the Tribes. The murals are a remarkable study in variations of ancient script, archaeological finds in the shape of coins and lamps, beautiful verses of the Bible, the tribes and their symbols. They were designed and executed in Haifa, Israel, by Jacob Ben-Shalom. Mr. Ben-Shalom was a neighbor of my wife's cousin, Yvette Arazi, in Haifa. He was born in 1932 in Jerusalem, where his father is a wise man carrying on the tradition of a dynasty of Persian kabbalists. A graduate of the Bezalel School of Art, Mr. Ben-Shalom is represented by major works throughout Israel and Africa.

Among these projects are parts of the Parliament in Lagos, Nigeria; arks for the Spanish synagogue in Haifa; and parts of synagogues at the Technion in Haifa, the Nazareth synagogue, and the Tel Aviv synagogue. In addition, Ben-Shalom has made the main door of the church

THE CHAPELS
AND REMEMBRANCES

Jacob Ben-Shalom

at Nazareth, parts of a mosque at the University of Tanzania, and the ceiling of the office of the president of Israel.

Mr. Ben-Shalom now resides in Jerusalem. On my initial visit to his studio, I immediately was captivated by his work. I proposed several themes; after a week of daily meetings for discussions and reviewing sketches, I decided on the subject that was finally produced and engaged the artist for the commission.

The two murals are put together in a horizontal arrangement of eight panels on each wall. The descriptions that follow refer to the horizontal panels; number one is the highest and eight is the lowest. Both one and eight are copies of ancient menorahs designed according to archaeological finds of ancient synagogues in Israel.

The Wall of the Coins. The Wall of the Coins bears an inscription from the last chapter of the Book of Psalms, Psalm 150:

Wall of the Coins

2 Praise ye the Lord. Praise God in His sanctuary; Praise Him in the firmament of His power.
3 Praise Him for His mighty acts; Praise Him according to His abundant greatness. Praise Him with the sound of the
4 horn; Praise Him with the harp and lyre. Praise Him with the timbrel
5 And dance; Praise Him with stringed instruments and the pipe. Praise Him
6 with the clear-toned cymbals; praise Him with the loud-sounding
7 cymbals. Let everything that hath breath praise the Lord. Praise ye the Lord.

The numerals both here and on the Wall of the Tribes, refer to the panels on the murals. The words are written in various scripts. The upper three panels are in the script of the Dead Sea Scrolls, discovered in the Judean desert. The middle panels use Hebrew scripts discovered in the ruins of the Second Temple. The lower scripts are of ancient Canaanite origin, changed by conquerors into Roman-Latin writings.

The coins surmounted on this panel are designed according to finds from the time of the Bar Kokhba revolt in the years 132 and 135 C.E. They are in denominations of silver tetradrachms and copper dinars and perutot, and bear the names of two government leaders—"Shimon the President" and "El'azar the Kohen." As there was no Josephus to describe the second great Jewish uprising against Rome under the able leadership of Bar Kokhba, recorded sources for these events are scarce.

The few writings available are the papyri found in the Judean

desert, the Talmud, and some meager information surviving from the
works of the Roman historian Dio Cassius. The most vivid evidence is,
therefore, the coinage of Bar Kokhba. The subjects of the coins are
partly national and partly religious, symbolizing the renewal of the
work on the Holy Temple and the Jewish nation reborn as the land
of Israel.

The top center coin represents the holy shrine, as does one on the
lower panel a little to the left of center. The vase on the coin in the
middle panel and one on the lower left panel show the palm branch,
lulav, etrog, and a cluster of grapes as ornaments of ancient Jewish art.
The harp on the left-hand panel, one up from the bottom, together
with the trumpets directly above that coin, symbolizes the musical
instruments. The palm tree on the middle of the right side, together
with the harp and the trumpets, symbolizes the land of Israel.

All these objects appear regularly in Jewish art. Most of the coins
were struck on the backs of Roman coins because of the lack of metal
and also for political reasons—as an insult to the Roman authorities,
and to demonstrate Jewish national independence.

The Wall of the Tribes.   The Wall of the Tribes has the complete
chapter 133 of the Book of Psalms:

2   A pilgrim song of David. Behold, how good
3   and how pleasant it is for brethren to dwell together in unity!
    It is like (goodly) oil
4   upon the head, that floweth down upon the beard; even Aaron's
    beard which cometh down
5   upon the skirt of his garments: Like the dew of Hermon,
6   that falleth upon the mountains of Zion; for there
7   the Lord commanded the blessing, even life for evermore.

Wall of the Tribes

On this mural there are also three different scripts. The upper portion
is a Hebrew script; the middle portion is an ancient Hebrew-Canaanite-
Sidonian script that was the international script of those times. The
lower portion is the script used at the time of the Second Temple.

The Wall of the Tribes has a plaque for each tribe with its name
and emblem and a pertinent sentence from the Bible. The tribes are
arranged as follows (reading from left to right at the upper level):

Naphtali, Asher, and Issachar.
The next level of three: Gad, Dan, Benjamin.
The next level of two: Zebulun and Joseph.
The bottom level: Reuben, Simeon, Levi, and Judah.

The individual tribal plaques have the following symbols and phrases from the Bible connecting each with the particular tribe:

1. *Naphtali*
A deer. "Naphtali is a hind [deer] let loose" [Gen. 49:21].

2. *Asher*
A tree. "As for Asher, his bread shall be fat" [Gen. 49:20].

3. *Issachar*
A flower. "And the children of Issachar, men that had understanding of the times" [I Chron. 12:33].

4. *Gad*
Three tents. "Gad, a troop shall troop upon him; but he shall troop upon their heel" [Gen. 49:19].

5. *Dan*
Scales of justice. "Dan shall judge his people" [Gen. 49:16].

6. *Zebulun*
A trireme. "And he shall be a shore for ships" [Gen. 49:13].

7. *Joseph*
A sheaf of wheat. "Blessed of the Lord shall be his land" [Deut. 33:13].

8. *Benjamin*
A wolf. "In the morning he devoureth the prey" [Gen. 49:27].

9. *Reuben*
Flower buds. "Let Reuben live" [Deut. 33:6].

10. *Simeon*
A building façade [a temple? a Jerusalem gate?]. "The tribes of Israel shall be together" [Deut. 33:5].

11. *Levi*
A hoshen [priest's breastplate]. "They shall teach Jacob Thine ordinances, and Israel Thy law" [Deut. 33:10].

12. *Judah*
A lion. "Judah is a lion's whelp" [Gen. 49:9].

The murals are made of alpaca—a mixture of copper, brass, lead, solder, and silver. They have been lacquered to prevent oxidation. They are one-half millimeter in thickness, backed on polyester and wood.

Mr. Ben-Shalom's hope, in completing these panels for Beth El Synagogue, is that the Third Temple will be built in Jerusalem.

WALLPAPER. The wallpaper of the Levenson Chapel was printed from the same screen and design as the wallpaper in the Goldberger Chapel and in the lower lobby, described below.

MENORAHS. The menorahs and the seating of the Levenson Chapel were taken from the original Goldberger Chapel. This latter Chapel, built in the first stage of our complex, was moved to a new location in the final stage.

THE STARS. The upper rear wall contains ninety-five stars. For over forty years of worship at our Union Avenue synagogue, the ends of each pew row were decorated by a six-pointed star. When the building was sold, the stars, along with other decorations, were removed at my direction. The stars were installed in the rear wall of the Levenson Chapel and are a permanent reminder of the decades of worship at Union Avenue.

A careful examination of the stars revealed that the two triangles were intertwined. The intertwined six-pointed star is known as Solomon's Seal, and the level-plane six-pointed star, as the Star of David. Research into the subject explained part of the story as to where and when these names originated.

The six-pointed Star of David on a level plane and the star with the triangles intertwined (Solomon's Seal), as well as the five-pointed star, all originated as geometric symbols used by the Greeks, whose astrologists believed that these symbols possessed divine powers. The use of the three devices was not significant in Judaism two thousand years ago, nor was either of the six-pointed stars the emblem of the Jewish people. Excavations of synagogues and burial places rarely show the stars, and then only in conjunction with other insignia.

The second-century synagogue at Capernaum has a six-pointed star and a five-pointed star, both given equal treatment with many other symbols, including a swastika. The only pre–seventeenth century tomb with a Star of David is one from the sixth century that was unearthed at Taranto, Italy; but even there the star had no particular significance as a religious object.

The menorah was the Shield of David and emblem of Judaism during the Second Commonwealth period and for many centuries thereafter. The stars were used by Jews, Arabs, and Christians alike, with no emphasis by any of them. The star was considered a talisman against evil spirits. Consequently, it was found on mezuzot and other amulets. Thus, the star began its "Jewish career" not as a symbol of our monotheistic faith but as a protection against evil, and this remained its primary meaning until about one hundred years ago.

The six-pointed star came to be publicized as a symbol of Judaism

through a misinterpretation in the writings of Rabbi Isaac Luria (known as the Ari), the sixteenth-century kabbalist. Rabbi Luria, in his *Tree of Life*, writes that the Seder plate should be arranged in two triangles, one above the other, comprising the bone, egg, herb, horseradish, parsley, and haroset. Each portion represented a different kabbalistic emanation. However, when artists began to represent the Seder plate, they drew Rabbi Luria's Seder plate with the triangles over each other, thus creating a six-pointed star rather than two separate triangles. This error has continued until the present day, and many contemporary Seder plates are designed with the six-pointed star.

The terms *Shield of David* and *Solomon's Seal* were developed from legends. In the thirteenth century, Eleazar of Worms wrote about King David's golden shield, on which the "Great Name" was engraved by combining seventy-two holy names. Solomon's Seal originated with the description of a seal ring used by Solomon, also containing the "Great Name" of God. This was developed in great depth by Moslem writers. Another tradition, taught by Rabbi Isaac Arama in fifteenth-century Spain, states that the emblem of King David's shield was Psalm 67 in the shape of a menorah. This interpretation received widespread approval.

While the magical roots of the Shield of David never really found popular acceptance, the star's role as the official seal of a community launched it along the path to its current usage. In the year 1354 in Prague, Emperor Charles IV gave the Jews the freedom to bear a flag as a token of their stay in the city. The flag had a six-pointed star on it. Other Jewish communities in neighboring cities soon adopted it. In Hungary, in the fifteenth century, the Jewish community used two five-pointed stars on their flag; in Vienna, in the year 1655, a six-pointed star was used. The prime motive for the use of the star seems to have been the need of the Jewish people for a symbol comparable to Christianity's cross.

In 1897, at the First Zionist Congress in Basel, the star was adopted as the Zionist symbol. Some forty years later, the Shield of David took on a different meaning when Hitler made it the badge of millions of Jewish people on the road to eventual extermination. When the State of Israel was established in 1947, the government of Israel returned to the symbol in use two thousand years before and adopted the menorah as its official emblem.

THE GOLDBERGER CHAPEL

The Goldberger Chapel is located directly below the bimah of the main sanctuary. The two stained-glass columns of the sanctuary continue down to the floor of the chapel. Here, in this intimate room with a capacity of one hundred, daily services are conducted by the congregation and Sabbath morning services by the teenagers.

The eastern wall of the chapel is a representation of the upper portion of the Western Wall in Jerusalem. The ceiling has a recessed dome with a decorative motif of the two tablets of the Law, made of rolled zinc. The Eternal Light was designed by Paavo Tynell of Finland, one of the most renowned designers of lighting fixtures in the world.

There is also a recess for the Counting of the Omer.[1]

The ark is a simple wooden cabinet designed by Herbert Phillips, A.I.A., adorned by twelve pewter pieces representing the twelve tribes. The rear of the chapel has cabinets for storage of tallesim and tefillin. The wood used here, as well as most of the wood used in the building, is benge. The walls of the chapel are covered with Beth El's especially designed "Mahzor" wallpaper.

BETH EL'S MAHZOR WALLPAPER

Beth El's wallpaper was named after the festival prayerbook, or Mahzor. The design of the paper continued our program of introducing traditional objects into the decorations of our contemporary building. Several motifs for this design were taken from illustrations in various mahzorim, the oldest in the Mahzor Vitry.[2]

The wallpaper, covering the walls of the Goldberger and Levenson chapels and the lower lobby areas, was designed by Adriana Scalamandre Bitter, chief designer for the Scalamandre firm, which produces wallpaper, carpets, fabrics, and trimmings for homes, offices, and public buildings, as well as historical restorations such as the White House, Blair House, Monticello, and colonial Williamsburg.

Franco Scalamandre, the founder of the firm, was a graduate of the Polytechnical Institute of Naples. He and his wife, Flora, an artist, emigrated to the United States in 1927. Their daughter Adriana, born

[1] The Bible tells us in Leviticus 23:10–15, that the Omer was a sheaf cut in the barley harvest, offered at the Sanctuary before eating the grain of the new harvest. From the day after the Sabbath of the offering (the second day of Passover) the people are directed to keep a count of each day, for a period of seven weeks. The period ends with Shavuot (Feast of Weeks). The time for the counting is after the evening service. It is preceded by a special benediction. The standard formula, altered for each day, runs as follows: "Today is the 10th day, making one week and three days of the Omer." Originally joyful, this period became one of semi-mourning, as Jews suffered repeated tragedies during Sephirah (the Counting of the Omer).

[2] Written by Simhah b. Samuel of Vitry, France (ca. 1100). First published by Mekize Nordamim (Berlin 1889–1893), second edition (Nurnberg, 1923). Simon Hurwitz, ed.

Adriana Scalamandre Bitter

in 1939, grew up in an artistic environment because her parents did a great deal of their designing of silks at home. Adriana later studied at the Parsons School of Design and with a student of the neo-impressionist Georges Seurat, while helping her father at their mill.

In the Beth El wallpaper, the circular motif was taken from the first page of the Schocken Bible. In each circle of the page, there are scenes from biblical history. This Bible was written in southern Germany (ca. 1300) by a scribe named Hayyim (life). The original can be seen in the Schocken Library in Jerusalem.

The palm-tree design was taken from a detail in the mosaic floor of the fourth-century synagogue at Naro, Tunisia,[3] found on a coin dating from the Bar Kokhba revolt.

The fleur-de-lis was taken from the carvings of the gravestone of Samuel Texeira, 1717.[4] It was often used in carvings and illustrations in various mahzorim. It was also found on the "Yehud" silver coin of Persian period, sixth to fourth century B.C.E.

The grapes were taken from the frieze of a third-century synagogue at Khorazin in the Galilee.

The intercircular motifs of flowers and scrolls were taken from the wall decoration of the synagogue of Don Samuel ha-Levi Abulafia in Toledo, Spain (El Tránsito).

The lions date from the third century, a period in which the Jews entered upon an era of adventurous exploration of animal and human representations. The lion became very popular, and prominent lion figures were found in a Scroll of Esther from southern France, dating from the early sixteenth century.[5] A design of the lion in minuscular letters was found in a thirteenth-century manuscript, at the beginning of the Masorah to the Book of Ezekiel.[6]

The menorah is from an original stone imprint of a second-century menorah found in the synagogue at Hammat. A later version of this type (represented in the design) was found on a bronze lamp from Syria and also on a clay lamp from Israel, now in a private collection.[7] The same style is found in the mosaic floors of a number of ancient synagogues in Israel, among them the fourth-century synagogue near Kibbutz Nirim in the Negev.

The birds were taken from a page in the Laud Mahzor, which was written in southern Germany in the year 1290. This Mahzor, now in Oxford, England, in the Bodleian Library, has nineteen full-page illus-

[3] Hamman LIF, Tunisia, Cecil Roth, *Jewish Art* (New York: McGraw-Hill, 1961), p. 218.
[4] Ouderkerk Cemetery, Amsterdam.
[5] Roth Collection, Oxford.
[6] German manuscript now in National Library, Vienna.
[7] Collection of A. Reifenberg, Jerusalem.

trations. Mrs. Bitter took the symbol of the birds from one of the pages for Shavuot, the giving of the Torah, and used it on our wallpaper design. All the human faces are distorted to animal figures, as was customary with Jewish artists of the period. These dragonlike, mythical birds, Bar Yokhani (Ziz), are often found in ancient Bibles and prayerbooks and symbolize the last days of judgment. Ziz was the legendary king of the birds, as monstrous in size as Leviathan; his ankles rest on the earth and his head reaches to the sky. Like Leviathan and Behemoth, he was a delicacy to be served to the pious at the end of time.[8]

REMEMBRANCES

MEMORIAL WALLS. There are two memorial walls flanking the entrance to the daily chapel. Each wall has a word designed in bronze in the shape of a torch, silhouetted with recessed lighting. On one wall is the word *Yizkor* ("He will remember") and on the other, *Kaddish* ("sanctification," the title of the traditional memorial prayer). Names of departed ones are inscribed individually in uniform-size, cut-bronze letters.

The walls were designed and executed by the Israeli artist Ami Shamir. Born in 1932 in Tel Aviv, Mr. Shamir has worked in a wide variety of media, including sculpture, painting, glass, and textiles, from design through fabrication and installation. In the theater, he has done costume designing and created stage sets for six of Israel's most important theaters.

Mr. Shamir has received commissions for murals in public buildings in Israel and abroad, some of which are the Weizmann Institute in Rehovot, the Uris Theater in New York, and the stained-glass memorial at the Virginia Military Institute, New Market, Virginia. He has designed and supervised the Israel pavilion for ten international expositions and fairs. In 1968 Mr. Shamir was invited by the University of Illinois to participate as a fellow at the Center of Advanced Study. He has also had numerous individual exhibitions and has participated in group showings throughout the world.

THE HALL OF REMEMBRANCE. The Hall of Remembrance consists of three walls: the Wall of Officers, the Donor's Wall, and the Panels of Honor, all designed by Mr. Shamir.

The Wall of Officers. The Wall of Officers is made of white

[8] From Bezalel Narkiss, *Hebrew Illuminated Manuscripts* (Jerusalem: Encyclopaedia Judaica, 1969).

Yizkor

Kaddish

carrara marble with a feature design of ancient Judaic symbols. It lists the officers of Beth El Synagogue from its beginnings.

The Donor's Wall. The Donor's Wall is also made of white carrara marble with a feature design of ancient symbols. Here, the names of the donors to the Beth El building funds are listed.

The Panels of Honor. The third wall is comprised of five silk-screened panels of benge wood listing the rabbis of Beth El, our annual guests of honor, the officers and directors of the year 1971–72 (the year of dedication), the building committee of the sanctuary wing, the list of names taken from the Union Avenue Synagogue windows, and the officers listed in the lobby of the old synagogue.

When our congregation voted to move uptown, I incorporated in the motion a commitment to reenshrine in the new building all the dedications and memorials from the old structure. The Hall of Remembrance fulfilled the promise.

The proverbs or quotations heading each of the walls were selected by Rabbi Melvin D. Sirner, Harvey Silton, and myself.

Donor's Wall

Wall of Officers

LISHKAT HASHSHA'IM AND GENIZAH

LISHKAT HASHSHA'IM

> The children of Israel brought a freewill offering unto the Lord;
> every man and woman, whose heart made them willing to bring for
> all the work, which the Lord had commanded by the hand of Moses
> to be made.[1]

The *Lishkat Hashsha'im* (secret chamber) at Beth El reinstitutes a
tradition that probably has not been observed in a synagogue anywhere
in the world in at least the last fifteen hundred years.

The Second Temple in Jerusalem had a special vault that received
anonymous donations for the support of the worthy poor. Since its
purpose was to shield both the givers and the receivers of charity, it was
called the "secret chamber." Into the secret chamber people dropped
silver and gold coins and vessels. Every thirty days the chamber was
opened by the priests, and its contents were reserved for the needy. The
donors did not know the identity of the recipients, and the beneficiaries
did not know the identity of their benefactors. What remained after
the distribution to the poor was appropriated to *bedek ha-bayit*, the
fund for "repairs of the sanctuary." [2]

The Lishkat Hashsha'im at Beth El faces the entrance to the Goldberger Chapel. A bronze plaque, 20 inches by 24 inches, with a slot for
contributions, it was designed by Rothschild and Lippmann of Tel
Aviv and cast by Nahum Weiss of Azur, Israel.

[1] Ex. 35:29.
[2] Mishnah, Shekalim 5:6.

I uncovered the idea for the Lishkat Hashsha'im while researching in an old encyclopedia. Eminent rabbis and scholars were consulted, but few had even a fleeting knowledge of the subject, so I conducted intensive studies in Israel at the various university libraries and at the library of the Jewish Theological Seminary in New York.

After Messrs. Rothschild and Lippmann were engaged, they added to my research and designed the oblong-shaped Lishkat Hashsha'im with the following features:

1. Ornamental circles in the upper portion, taken from decorations in an ancient synagogue at Ashkelon.

2. Coins, the obverse and reverse of a shekel, one of the coins of the Maccabeans, with the inscription "Shekel Israel" and "Holy Jerusalem."

3. A shofar, a symbol of plenty, according to a source in the Talmud, and thus used as a receptacle for collecting charity money.

4. A pomegranate, a Jewish symbol of wisdom and plenty.

The plaque carries the words *Lishkat Hashsha'im* and in English, "Secret Charity Chamber, a Heritage from the Second Temple in Jerusalem." There is also a quotation from Bava Batra 10:2: "He giveth and knoweth not to whom, he receiveth and knoweth not from whom."

The artists Gerd Rothschild and Ze'ev Lippmann met while studying graphic design at the Bezalel School of Art in Jerusalem. Rothschild, born in 1919, and Lippmann, born in 1921, left their native Germany as young boys and arrived in Israel in the early 1930s. In 1939 their student friendship grew into a permanent partnership, now called Studio Roli.

After World War II, Rothschild and Lippmann designed the only book published in Israel on the subject of Hebrew artistic lettering. Mr. Rothschild has taught graphic design at the Bezalel School. Since 1956, he and Mr. Lippmann have become prominent in the field of designing medals and stamps for Israel and other countries. They have designed the International Bible Contest coins: the Eilat Jubilee coin; one side of all the present-day coins of the State of Israel; over twenty-four of Israel's stamps, including "Knesset," "Masada," "Victory," "Keren Hayesod," and the landscape series of 1972.

Studio Roli has also designed posters, trademarks and tour emblems, and the official state emblem, "25 Years Israel." They have won over ninety-five prizes in both Israeli and international competitions.

LISHKAT HASHSHA'IM
AND GENIZAH

The Beth El *genizah* (hiding place or repository) continues an ancient tradition whereby old copies of the Torah and time-worn Hebrew books were either buried in the cemetery or stored away in the storeroom of a synagogue. The Talmud states specifically: "If a Scroll of the Law has two mistakes per page, it must be corrected; if three mistakes, it must be hidden away." [3]

THE CAIRO GENIZAH. For the last two centuries, the genizah of the Ezra Synagogue of Fostat (old Cairo), Egypt, has attracted the attention of world scholars.[4] The Ezra Synagogue, originally a church dedicated to St. Michael, became a synagogue after the conquest of Egypt by Chosroes II of Persia in the year 616.

Over the course of more than a thousand years, an enormous wealth of material was stored in this genizah, but it was only uncovered about two hundred years ago. In 1896 Dr. Solomon Schechter brought this literary treasure to the attention of the world when he acquired over 100,000 leaves from the genizah.[5] In addition, many more documents from the genizah, including letters by Maimonides and other scholars, found their way into libraries throughout the world, where the work of translation still goes on and will probably continue for several centuries.

The Beth El genizah, located in the boardroom, is used for storing worn-out prayerbooks, tallesim, and other religious articles. Covering the genizah are two bronze plates measuring 26 by 29 inches. These were designed in Tel Aviv by Rothschild and Lippmann. The design presents the feeling of scrolls and carries a pertinent quotation—"Sacred writings . . . may not be destroyed"—from the Mishnah, Shabbat 16:1.

The bronze covering plates were cast and fabricated by Nahum Weiss. Mr. Weiss, who was born in Russia in 1924, studied sculpture in Siberia. He emigrated to Israel in 1948. After two years of military service in the Israel Defense Forces, he established himself as a metal worker and sculptor with leading Israeli artists. As such, he does the actual translating into three dimensions, the sculpturing, and the final casting.

[3] Menahot 29.

[4] Harry M. Rabinowicz, *The Jewish Literary Treasures of England and America* (New York: Thomas Yoseloff, 1962).

[5] Dr. Solomon Schechter (1848–1915), Rumanian-born scholar and lecturer at Cambridge, came to America in 1901, accepting the post of president of the Jewish Theological Seminary. He served in this capacity until his death. He was instrumental in the founding of the United Synagogue of America and is considered the chief architect of Conservative Judaism in the United States.

In Israel his works can be seen at Yad Vashem, the Hilton Hotel in Tel Aviv, and the Yiftah War Memorial. Several of his sculptures have also found their way to the United States. He has been employed by Naftali Bezem, Marcel Janco, Dani Karavan, and others.

Mr. Weiss has been translating the work of Rothschild and Lippmann into three-dimensional sculpture and final casting for many years. In finishing the genizah plates, he used a polished letter effect with a slightly oxidized background.

My discovery of this group of artists originated with a glance at the sports pages of the *New York Times* in early 1969. There I saw a three-column article and a photograph showing how sports and freedom had been combined to provide the motif for the Israel medals struck for the eighth Maccabiah games, to be held that summer. The designs attracted me as a means of expression suitable for the genizah and lishkat ideas. Thomas V. Haney, coin editor of the *Times*, provided me with the names and addresses of the artists. This started a voluminous correspondence with Rothschild and Lippmann, leading to our commissioning them and to their introducing me to Nahum Weiss.

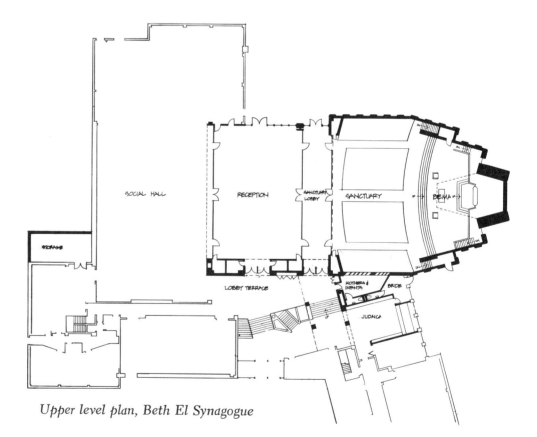

Upper level plan, Beth El Synagogue

WALL OF THE MARTYRS

I LIFT UP MY EYES TO THE HILLS.
FROM WHENCE DOES MY HELP COME?
MY HELP COMES FROM THE LORD,
WHO MADE HEAVEN AND EARTH.
                              —*Psalms 121:1–2*

Jews have suffered persecution and martyrdom without parallel in the history of any other people. Nevertheless, the world's historians, scholars, and artists—whether by chance or design—have, for the most part, chosen to ignore or to give but cursory attention to this tragic saga.

Even the Hitler Holocaust, so enormous in its dimensions, so obscene in its horror, standing forever as an indictment of Western civilization, has now been relegated to an obscure footnote on the vast pages of world history.

Our Jewish martyrs cry out for an end to this neglect. Their cries find expression in the monumental bronze mural, *Wall of the Martyrs*, sculpted by Luise Kaish. The wall depicts major episodes in the more than two thousand years of Jewish martyrdom.

Unique in theme, *Wall of the Martyrs* is the only work of such scope and dimension to have been commissioned by a synagogue on the American continent.

The idea for this project originated early in my life. As a youth I was appalled by the neglect of Jewish history and the lack of mention of both the great achievements and the persecution of our people—both in textbooks and in the history courses of the public school system.

Many years later, when I became chairman of Beth El's building committee, I conceived the idea of a mural on martyrdom to educate our people about our heritage, the monstrous crimes perpetrated against our ancestors, and the heroic stand taken by our people to affirm their faith.

My plan was to engage a scholar to research the subject, and then engage an artist to translate this material into a moving and inspiring

Luise Kaish

work of art. I asked the late Dr. Abraham J. Heschel, a dear friend of ours, to recommend a scholar.[1] While aiding me in the selection process, which lasted over a year, Dr. Heschel repeatedly insisted: "This wrong must be corrected. . . . You must do it."

With his encouragement, the work went forward. Finally, Dr. Aaron Kirschenbaum, a rabbi at the Jewish Theological Seminary, to whom I was referred by Dr. Heschel, was engaged to research the subject.[2] Rabbi Edmund Winter, assistant rabbi at Beth El from 1970 to 1972, contributed additional writings. I, too, worked in the areas of research, artistic media, and the selection of the artist.

After a prolonged period of investigation, during which I went through studies of many art forms, including oil, stained glass, wood carving, and tapestry, I decided on bronze as the most effective medium for this project. Then followed my search for sculptors. I had already viewed with positive reactions three works by Luise Kaish. To locate her I called the Jewish Museum, the Kaish apartment in New York (which had been sublet to someone else), and a sister in Forest Hills; I finally found Luise at the American Academy in Rome, Italy, where she was a scholar-in-residence. When I visited Luise at the studio in Rome, surrounded by some of her work, I instinctively knew that she could successfully transpose my idea to reality.

Luise Kaish was born in Atlanta, Georgia, and studied at Syracuse University, Escuela de Pintura y Escultura, Escuela de las Artes del Libro, and Taller Gráfico—in Mexico.

She has been the recipient of the Syracuse University graduate fellowship, a Louis Comfort Tiffany grant, a John Simon Guggenheim fellowship, the Rome Prize, and a Rome fellowship.

Her commissions have come from Syracuse University; Container Corporation of America; temples in Rochester (New York), Westport (Connecticut), Wilmington (Delaware), and Essex County (New Jersey); Holy Trinity Mission Seminary in Silver Springs, Maryland; the Jewish Museum in New York; and the Union of American Hebrew Congregations in Jerusalem.

She has had one-woman exhibitions at the Rochester Memorial Art Gallery, the New York Sculpture Center, the New York Staempfli Gallery, the St. Paul, Minnesota, Art Center, and the Jewish Museum in New York.

[1] Dr. Abraham J. Heschel (1907–1973), prophet, philosopher, and scholar, was born in Poland to a Hasidic family. He settled in the United States in 1940, lecturing at Hebrew Union College, then at the Jewish Theological Seminary. He became one of the most influential modern philosophers of religion in the United States.

[2] Rabbi Kirschenbaum is now professor of Jewish law, and head of the department of Jewish law at the University of Tel Aviv.

Mrs. Kaish used the background material provided to her and added her own research, both in the United States and in Rome at the Vatican Library. I traveled to Rome from time to time, as work on the wall relief progressed, to approve the work in its various stages.

The eight panels of the wall produce an overall dimension of 17 by 7½ feet. The casting was by Fonderìa Artìstica Bruni of Rome, Italy.

Dr. Avram Kampf, professor of art history at Haifa University, and advisor and consultant to the Jewish Museum in New York, states, in a Jewish Museum catalogue:

> There is a strong religious vein which runs through the work of Luise Kaish and which sets her apart from the sculptors of her generation. This religious element is a fundamental component of her work based on her own experience of the world and her personal attitude toward it.
>
> In her art, she conveys the decisive moments in the life of man as he encounters the Holy. The image of man is represented in a primary state of inwardness, confronting the Divine in a fateful meeting and in a continuous dialogue between himself and an unfathomable world.

Noble in concept, inspired in design, and gifted in execution, the *Wall of the Martyrs* by Luise Kaish has gained recognition as a pilot work, opening new avenues of artistic expression in both history and religion. Beth El Synagogue justifiably is proud to serve as the repository for this eloquent statement of the Jewish experience.

Luise Kaish describes the wall as follows:

THE ETERNAL MARTYR

A figure symbolic of the prophets of Israel who listened to the Voice of God and, thus inspired, went forth to speak out against iniquity. The outstretched arm, the open mouth, the stance of the figure, are intended to show the quality of ecstasy as seen against the hovering spirit of the angel, the messenger.

THE FLIGHT FROM JERUSALEM

The flight from Jerusalem in 586 B.C.E. was inspired by the first passages from Lamentations in which Jeremiah wrote:

How doth the city sit solitary,

The Eternal Martyr

The Flight from Jerusalem

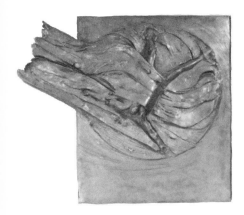

The Ten Martyrs

Masada

The Crusades

That was full of people!
How she is become as a widow!

The Holy City, razed by the Babylonians, is shown engulfed in flames. The old men in their prayer shawls, the young men, and the woman with child, flee the desolation to death, exile, or slavery.

THE TEN MARTYRS

The agony and strength of Rabbi Hananya ben Teradyon, one of the Ten Martyrs, recalled in the poem "Eleh Ezkerah" ("These men do I recall") is recited on the Day of Atonement. Wrapped in the Torah from which he had been teaching, he was placed on a pyre of green brushwood, his chest drenched with water to prolong his agony, and burned alive. He is depicted here defiant, reaching forth from the circle of flames which consume him. Asked by his disciples: "Master, what do you see?" he replied, "I see parchment burning while the letters of the Torah soar upward."

MASADA

The formidable face of rock, Masada, is shown rising amidst the beautiful and desolate wasteland surrounded by natural mysteries of the Dead Sea. Most Jews are now familiar with the story of the heroic group who sought refuge and fought here. As a theme for this wall it is also symbolic of the countless times during successive occupations of the Homeland and centuries of exile of the Jew when a group, large or small, banded together to resist religious tyranny and died in a reaffirmation of their Faith.

THE CRUSADES

The Crusades lasted almost four centuries, from 1096 to 1475 C.E. For the Church and the ignorant populace, the Jew, characterized eternally by his willingness to suffer death rather than renounce his faith in God, remained an enigma and as a consequence a threat to their essential teachings. How did the Jew, unlike other conquered and subjugated peoples, manage to survive and retain his beliefs? The fifth panel recalls the persecutions during the Crusades. It encompasses those centuries when power and conquest, in the

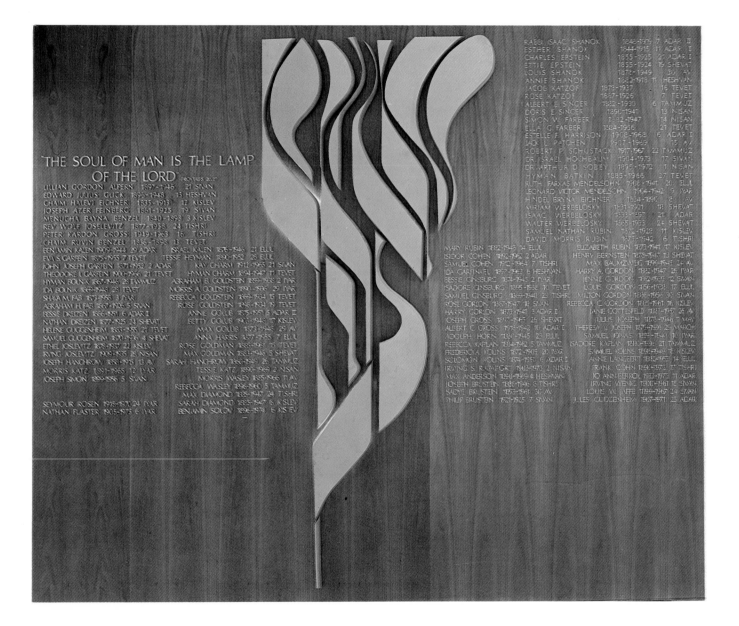

THE SOUL OF MAN IS THE LAMP
OF THE LORD PROVERBS 20:27

LILLIAN GORDON ALPERN 1897-1946 21 SIVAN
EDWARD JULIUS GLICK 1895-1948 15 HESHVAN
CHAIM HALEVI EICHNER 1835-1913 12 KISLEV
JOSEPH AZER FEINBERG 1861-1925 19 SIVAN
MENUCHA BAYNA BENZEL 1840-1893 3 KISLEV
REV WOLF JOSELEVITZ 1877-1938 24 TISHRI
PETER KARDON GROSS 1949-1963 16 TISHRI
CHAIM RUVIN BENZEL 1835-1898 13 TEVET
BENJAMIN KALEN 1909-1944 29 ADAR   ISRAEL KALEN 1876-1946 21 ELLUL
EVA S GARFEIN 1875-1955 7 TEVET   TESSIE HEYMAN 1890-1952 25 ELUL
JOHN JOSEPH GARFEIN 1871-1962 2 ADAR   KAY CHARM 1912-1965 21 SIVAN
THEODORE I GARFEIN 1900-1956 21 TEVET HYMAN CHARM 1894-1947 11 TEVET
HYMAN BOLNIK 1867-1946 28 TAMMUZ   ABRAHAM B GOLDSTEIN 1859-1938 2 IYAR
IDA BOLNIK 1869-1948 25 TEVET   MORRIS A GOLDSTEIN 1890-1936 29 IYAR
SHAYA M FAS 1871-1958 3 IYAR   REBECCA GOLDSTEIN 1869-1944 15 TEVET
ABRAHAM H FAS 1867-1926 5 SIVAN   ROSE GOLDSTEIN 1896-1964 19 TEVET
BESSIE DREIZEN 1886-1951 6 ADAR I   ANNIE GOLUB 1875-1951 5 ADAR II
NATHAN DREIZEN 1877-1925 24 SHEVAT   BETTY GOLUB 1903-1946 17 KISLEV
HELENE GUGGENHEIM 1881-1955 21 TEVET MAX GOLUB 1873-1948 29 AV
SAMUEL GUGGENHEIM 1870-1936 4 SHEVAT ANNA HARRIS 1877-1955 7 ELUL
ETHEL JOSLEVITZ 1878-1937 22 KISLEV ROSE GOLDMAN 1885-1961 15 TEVET
IRVING JOSLEVITZ 1903-1938 25 NISAN MAX GOLDMAN 1883-1946 5 SHEVAT
JOSEPH HANCHROW 1855-1975 13 AV   SARAH HANCHROW 1860-1949 26 TAMMUZ
MORRIS KATZ 1891-1965 12 IYAR   TESSIE KATZ 1890-1969 2 NISAN
JOSEPH SIMON 1899-1956 5 SIVAN   MORRIS WASLEY 1885-1966 11 AV
                                     REBECCA WASLEY 1898-1960 5 TAMMUZ
SEYMOUR ROSEN 1918-1970 24 IYAR   MAX DIAMOND 1885-1947 24 TISHRI
NATHAN FLASTER 1905-1975 6 IYAR   SARAH DIAMOND 1885-1947 6 KISLEV
                                     BENJAMIN SOLOV 1896-1974 6 KISLEV

RABBI ISAAC SHANOK   1848-1919 7 ADAR II
ESTHER SHANOK   1844-1915 11 ADAR I
CHARLES EPSTEIN   1855-1915 21 ADAR I
ETTIE EPSTEIN   1855-1924 19 SHEVAT
LOUIS SHANOK   1872-1949 30 AV
ANNIE SHANOK   1862-1918 11 HESHVAN
JACOB KATZOF   1873-1937 16 TEVET
ROSE KATZOF   1897-1926 7 TEVET
ALBERT E SINGER   1882-1930 6 TAMMUZ
DORIS E SINGER   1890-1941 13 NISAN
SIMON W FARBER   1882-1947 14 NISAN
ELLA G FARBER   1884-1956 21 TEVET
ESTELLE F HARRISON   1908-1968 6 ADAR I
JACK L PATCHEN   1907-1963 15 AV
ROBERT P SCHUSTACK 1917-1967 22 TAMMUZ
DR ISRAEL HOCHBAUM 1904-1973 17 SIVAN
DR ARTHUR D SOBER   1895-1972 1 NISAN
HYMAN BATKIN   1885-1966 27 TEVET
RUTH FARKAS MENDELSOHN 1908-1941 20 ELUL
LEONARD VICTOR MENDELSOHN 1904-1942 9 IYAR
HINDEL BRYNA EICHNER 1854-1890 8 AV
MIRIAM WERBELOSKY   1831-1921 18 SHEVAT
ISAAC WERBELOSKY   1833-1897 21 ADAR
WALTER WERBELOSKY   1865-1933 24 SHEVAT
SAMUEL NATHAN RUBIN 1872-1928 11 KISLEV
DAVID MORRIS RUBIN 1875-1942 6 TISHRI

MARY RUBIN 1882-1945 14 ELUL   ELIZABETH RUBIN 1873-1941 17 KISLEV
ISIDOR COHEN 1892-1962 2 ADAR   HENRY BERNSTEIN 1878-1947 13 SHEVAT
SAMUEL COHEN 1912-1964 7 TISHRI   MAX BAUMZWEIG 1899-1945 24 AV
IDA GARFINKEL 1897-1963 6 HESHVAN   HARRY A GORDON 1882-1947 26 IYAR
BESSIE GINSBURG 1874-1945 2 IYAR   JENNIE GORDON 1862-1939 12 SIVAN
ISADORE GINSBURG 1895-1938 10 TEVET LOUIS GORDON 1856-1928 17 ELUL
SAMUEL GINSBURG 1869-1940 23 TISHRI MILTON GORDON 1886-1956 30 SIVAN
ROSE GORDON 1867-1947 18 SIVAN   REBECCA C GORDON 1885-1961 16 KISLEV
HARRY GORDON 1873-1941 3 ADAR I   JANIE GOTTESFELD 1883-1947 25 AV
JOSEPH GROSS 1897-1965 26 SHEVAT   JULIUS JOSEPH 1878-1946 1 MAY
ALBERT C GROSS 1918-1942 10 ADAR I   THERESA V JOSEPH 1873-1936 29 MARCH
ADOLPH HORN 1880-1945 23 ELUL   SAMUEL JONAS 1859-1940 18 IYAR
REBECCA KAPLAN 1884-1962 5 TAMMUZ   ISADORE KAPLAN 1880-1936 21 TAMMUZ
FREDERICK A KOLINS 1872-1905 20 IYAR SAMUEL KOLINS 1898-1949 18 KISLEV
SOLOMON KOLINS 1874-1957 6 ADAR I   ANNIE LANGBERT 1882-1953 14 ELUL
IRVING S RAPAPORT 1903-1973 2 NISAN FRANK COHEN 1890-1972 17 TISHRI
MAX ANDERSON 1890-1969 4 HESHVAN   JO ANN BERROL 1933-1973 11 ADAR
JOSEPH BRUSTEIN 1881-1946 6 TISHRI   IRVING WIENIG 1900-1961 24 SIVAN
SADYE BRUSTEIN 1885-1961 30 AV   LOUIS W JAFFE 1894-1967 24 SIVAN
PHILIP BRUSTEIN 1921-1925 7 SIVAN   JULES GUGGENHEIM 1907-1971 23 ADAR

XXVI   REMEMBRANCES   *Donors' Wall*

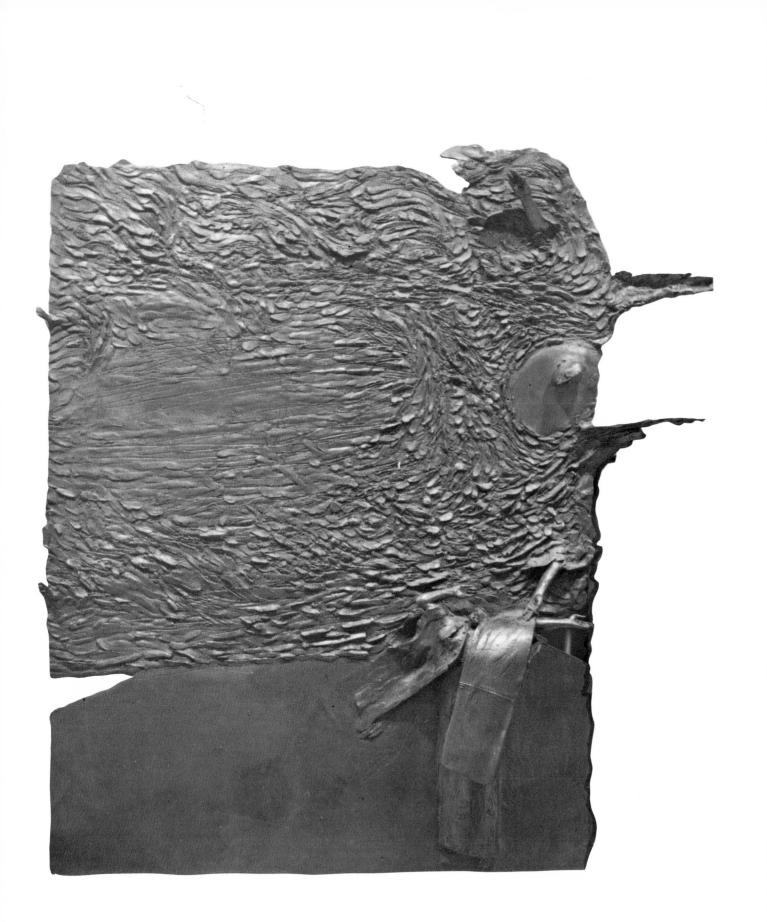

XXXII WALL OF MARTYRS *The Eternal Martyr*

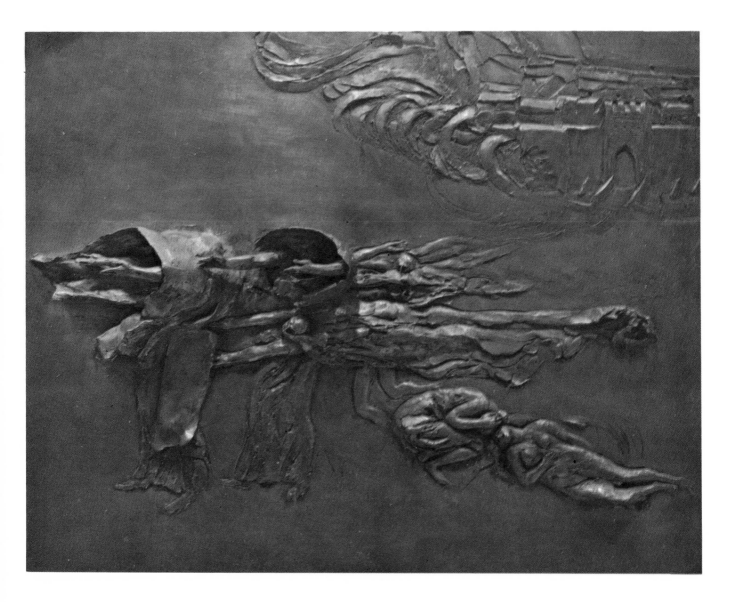

XXXIII WALL OF MARTYRS *The Flight From Jerusalem*

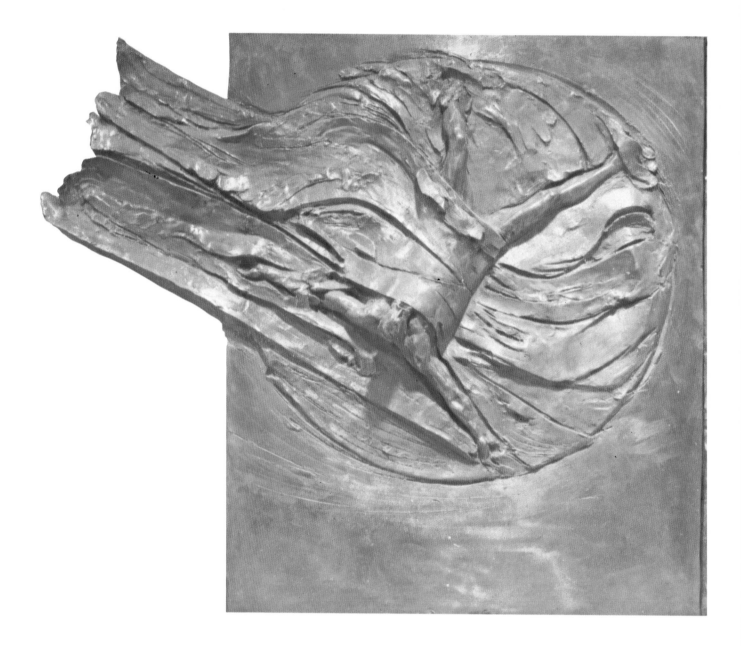

XXXIV WALL OF MARTYRS *The Ten Martyrs*

XXXV WALL OF MARTYRS *Masada*

XXXVI WALL OF MARTYRS *The Crusades*

XXXVII WALL OF MARTYRS *The Inquisition*

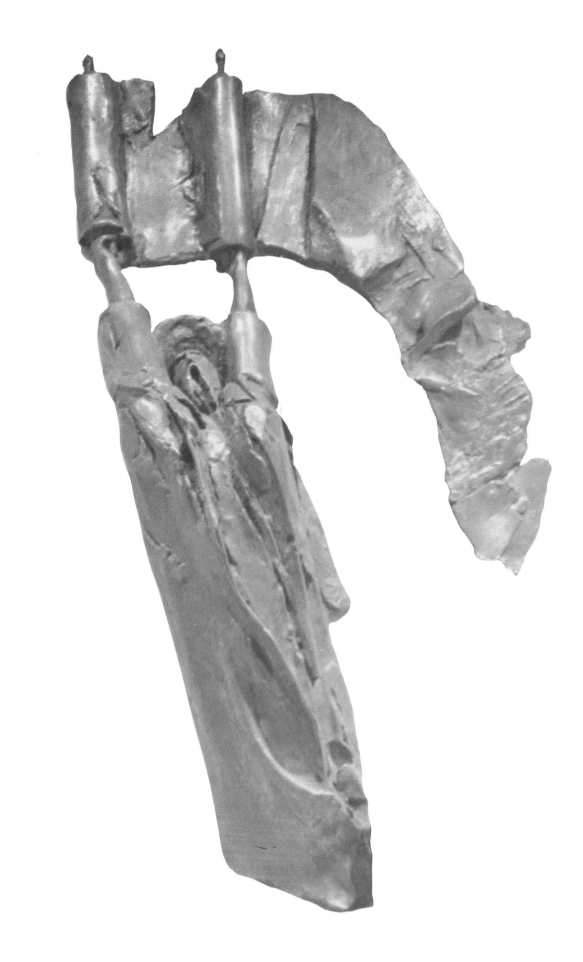

XXXVIII WALL OF MARTYRS *The Chmielnitzki Massacre*

XXXIX WALL OF MARTYRS *The Holocaust*

XL CHANDELIERS

guise of the charity of Jesus, were used systematically to reduce to ashes Jewish communities throughout Europe.

THE INQUISITION

This fever reached new heights during the time of the Inquisition. Church and State combined to eradicate the then culturally elite and influential Jewish communities of Spain and Portugal, ultimately reaching the New World. What is of particular significance during the years of the Inquisition was the extensive and perfidious use of mental and physical torture. This panel depicts the first episode in the formalized ritual of torture: the victim hung by his arms, his feet dragged down by weights, is interrogated by the clergy. In the panel the single figure, now frail but still resolute in the hands of his tormentors, reminds himself as he reminds us of the unnumbered thousands who were to perish at the hands of the Inquisitors.

The Inquisition

THE CHMIELNITZKI MASSACRE

Jews fleeing eastward settled in Germany, Poland, and Russia. Here arose the unique phenomenon of chassidism; that combination of delight in learning, that search for the spiritual manifestation of God in the pleasure of song and dance amidst misery and oppression. The Jew remained constant prey to destruction and annihilation. The panel depicts a typical massacre such as those of the infamous Chmielnitzki wherein is perpetrated the ultimate desecration for the pious Jew—the violation of the Sacred Scriptures. A Chassid is shown holding aloft the scrolls, torn, defiled, yet spiritually triumphant.

The Chmielnitzki Massacre

THE HOLOCAUST

The last panel represents the Holocaust in symbolic form. The crematorium door, now askew, its power to eradicate now spent, is surrounded by a field of flowers growing from the ashes of six million human beings. This toll, in terms of humanity, is the greatest in the history of man. The prayer of the Jew would be that, although still dispersed, the flowers rising anew on the deserts of Israel will re-affirm the Covenant between God and Abraham. It is our belief that should Israel be destroyed so will the world.

The Holocaust

The Jewish Museum of New York, upon learning of the *Wall*, asked permission to exhibit it prior to installation in our synagogue. This our board of trustees agreed to, and it was the principal work of art in a Luise Kaish show from October 1973 through April 1974. The *Wall* was then installed in our synagogue.

The *Wall of the Martyrs* was dedicated on November 3, 1974. A few weeks later, the bronze wall was awarded a citation in the category of Arts and Religion by the Fifth Annual Awards of the Council for the Arts in Westchester County.

Beth El was the first synagogue ever to receive such a citation. In its statement, the Council for the Arts in Westchester noted:

> After much research, you have courageously incorporated into the design of your new building many art forms: mosaics, ceramics, stained glass and metal sculpture. Although the concept of Jewish religious art is comparatively new because of the Talmudic admonition against depicting man, you have used the arts to commemorate the persecution of the Jews. The bronze plaques by Luise Kaish mirror the artist's own strong religious feeling to teach the story of the Jews from the flight from Jerusalem in 586 B.C. until the present time and the horrors of World War II.

The American Federation of Jewish Fighters, Camp Inmates, and Nazi Victims wrote to Mrs. Kaish in January of 1975:

> With our emotions high for the cause of remembrance, we like to express our recognition for your work, "The Wall of Martyrs," erected in the Beth El Synagogue-Center in New Rochelle, New York.
>
> The thought of remembrance in itself is great, but we are fortunate to have artists like you to be able to express the Jewish martyrdom throughout the ages in such an explicit way. We are deeply moved with your artistic ability to enable generations to read about Jewish martyrdom with your bronze mural. We will publicize, with your permission, the details of this monumental work for others to follow the example of the Beth El Synagogue in the New Rochelle community.

The *Wall* fulfilled an old urge for me, and I now only regret that its greatness is somewhat restricted in that it is housed in a suburban synagogue. However, I hope that we will be able to loan it out to museums for future exhibitions. It is one of the strongest and greatest artistic endeavors in our building and a noble tribute to Jewish martyrdom by a great artist, Luise Kaish.

ADDITIONAL FEATURES

Blessed be he who comes in the name of the Lord.
—*Psalm* 118:26

SOCIAL AREAS

The decorations of the social areas of the Beth El building, together with the color scheme for the entire building except the main sanctuary, were under the professional direction of Gertrude L. Schnee, N.S.I.D.

Gertrude Schnee received her B.A. from Hunter College, her M.A. at City College of New York, and is a graduate of the New York School of Interior Design. She has had twenty-five years of designing experience in residences, apartment houses, offices, and model apartments in the metropolitan New York area and in Florida. She is a member of the National Society of Interior Designers and the American Society of Interior Designers.

Mrs. Schnee worked in close concert with Edgar Tafel, our architect; with Jules G. Horton, lighting consultant; and with Mr. Tafel's two aides, Stanley B. Wright (coordinator of design) and R. Neill Gardner (decorator).

JACOBS LIBRARY

The library serves both the adult and school population. It consists of several thousand volumes. It also includes a collection of autographed letters and photographs of prominent Jews.

The reception hall is a contemporary room, decorated in a modern manner. It is served by the main kitchen, and its large glass doors lead to the Sukkah Garden.

FAYER BALLROOM

The ballroom is a glittering formal room with a capacity of 475 at a dinner. Seven different moldings were designed by Louis Maslow and Son, and made by the Millwork Center Company to frame the wall coverings. The drapery material and wall coverings were made by Scalamandre to match the carpet.

CHANDELIERS

The chandeliers used in the synagogue lobby, the reception hall, and the ballroom were made by E. Bakalowitz Sohne of Vienna, Austria.

There are three fixtures and six sconces in the ballroom, six fixtures in the reception room, and three in the synagogue lobby. The ballroom fixtures are each seven feet in diameter and five feet high, with eighty lamps and 3,512 pieces of crystal in each fixture. Among the in-depth studies was a sight-line study by Stanley B. Wright to determine whether the clearance from the bottom of the fixtures would be sufficient for those seated in the rear of the ballroom during High Holy Days services to view the ark in its entirety.

I first saw the products of Bakalowitz while visiting the Austrian building at the World's Fair in New York in 1964. When we were ready for the design of the chandeliers, I sketched out my ideas, had them drawn in more detail by Jenssen Kurnos Designs, with suggestions by Jules Horton and Edgar Tafel, and then commenced negotiations, making several visits to Bakalowitz in Vienna, in addition to telephone conversations, correspondence, and cable conferences. The Bakalowitz firm interpreted my thoughts very closely, and we were soon negotiating the usual terms, packing, shipping, and, in addition—since the work was being done overseas—the wire, sockets, bulbs, and rate of exchange, together with the type of hanging rods, lowering device, dimmers, import duties, and so forth. We specified a full hand- or wheel-cut crystal, not pressed.

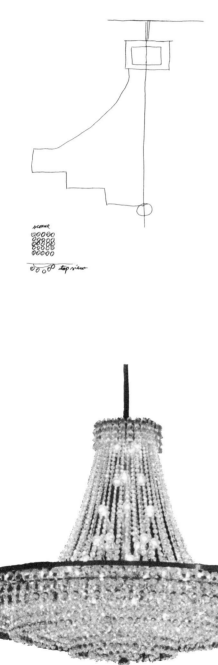

KASAKOVE YOUTH AUDITORIUM
AND MITCHELL YOUTH LOUNGE

These two areas on the lower level are both designed for the younger generation. The auditorium holds 450 at lectures. The lounge is furnished with couches and easy chairs, and with tables for pool, ping-pong, and other games.

WIENER LOUNGE

This is a small meeting and reception room adjacent to the main ballroom. It is exquisitely furnished with art from Israel. The chandelier was designed by Paavo Tynell.

KANNER KURZON MUSEUM

The museum was designed with recessed wall tracks and ceiling track lighting.

ISRAELI MARBLE AND LEGEND

The main lobby has a marble facia between two levels of the ceiling, carrying the welcoming phrase "And I shall dwell in the house of the Lord all the days of my life" (Ps. 23:6). This polished marble was imported from Israel.

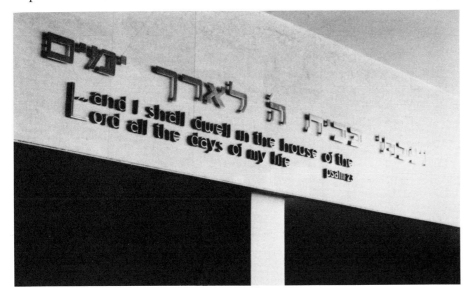

9 ADDENDA

GENERAL CONTRACTORS

The general contractors for the synagogue, Cuzzi Bros. & Singer, Inc., were a reliable and exacting contracting firm who were most helpful in many additional areas, particularly in the installation of our beautiful works of art.

A few weeks before the sanctuary dedication, they wrote to me:

Dear Mr. Batkin:

Cuzzi Bros. & Singer takes great pride in their participation in the construction of your Sanctuary and know that the Congregation will glory in its beauty and holiness in perpetuity.

It has been our privilege in years past to build many Houses of Worship for many faiths. We can think of none that surpasses yours in outstanding design and functional excellence.

We shall always remember with pleasure that no matter how difficult the problems, a satisfactory solution was reached because of the great good will and cooperation on the part of all concerned.

May the Lord's blessing rest on this edifice and all who labored with mind, heart and hand in its construction.

Alexander Singer

This book provides an appropriate occasion to pay tribute to Stanley Irving Batkin for the central role he played in directing every facet of Beth El's extensive expansion program.

Stanley planned our main sanctuary, contemporary in design, yet including traditional patterns and distinctive attributes of ancient synagogues. To that end, he examined classical and modern Jewish sources, the discoveries of archaeologists, and visited old synagogues in various parts of the world. He studied the Bible, the commentaries, and an endless list of other sources. On the basis of these studies, over a period of about twenty years, Stanley formulated the designs of our synagogue and communicated them to the architects to be built into our edifice.

So, too, the original and unique artwork gracing our synagogue was largely conceived by his fertile imagination and cultivated aesthetic sense. These concepts and themes were then transmitted to the artists whom he sought out and commissioned to appropriately translate and implement them.

I want to commend Stanley for preparing this book. Only one who agonized over every artifact herein described can authentically convey its essence and significance.

RABBI DAVID I. GOLOVENSKY

ACKNOWLEDGMENTS

The growth of Beth El from 1949 to 1970, when its building was completed, was the result of the dedicated efforts of many people and the generosity of its members.

At all times I had the complete cooperation and enthusiastic support of Rabbi David I. Golovensky, spiritual leader of the congregation from 1946 to 1976.

Rabbi Edmund Winter, Rabbi Melvin D. Sirner, Cantor Lawrence Avery, and Rev. Saul Friedler all assisted in researching and supplying quotations and valuable information. In addition, Rabbi Winter wrote portions of the story of the zodiac.

Executive director Harvey D. Silton provided rewriting, advice, and editing in many areas. Leah Silton assisted in the preparation of the index and in an advisory capacity.

Maxwell James, honorary president and elder statesman, Philip Kasakove, president from 1949 to 1959, Harry Wender, Sydney Mitchell, and Irving Sobel were dedicated leaders in the fund-raising area.

Daniel Locitzer, Alfred Goldstein, and Jack Rosen were prominent in the area of building, planning, and supervision. The associate chairmen of the building committee, Morton J. Baum, Jacob Goldner, Mortimer Grunauer, Moses Harary, Elliot Kahn, Manfred Moses, I. Milton Robbins, Martin Rosenfeld, and Myron Wander all aided in their particular fields of endeavor.

Valuable assistance was received from the library of the Jewish Theological Seminary of America, Professor Menachem Schmelzer, Adina Feldstern, Shamma Friedman, and Susan Winter.

The late revered Dr. Abraham J. Heschel gave assistance and encouragement for several important projects.

My good friend Harold Drimmer, with his rare span of knowledge, was always available to discuss projected ideas and lend his valuable advice.

The following people were all most cooperative and outstanding in their areas of achievement: architect Edgar Tafel and his associates Stanley Wright and R. Neill Gardner, lighting consultant Jules G. Horton, and decorator Gertrude L. Schnee, on the synagogue building; architect Herbert Phillips, who guided the first two building stages; Cuzzi Brothers & Singer, Inc., who built the sanctuary wing; and Blitman Construction Corp., who built the first two stages.

Ms. Sybil Kaufman of Jerusalem, Israel, Dr. Gloria Batkin Kahn of Scarsdale, New York, Alfred Fayer of New Rochelle, New York, Robert J. Milch of Stony Brook, New York, and Fay Tenzer of Jerusalem, all lent their expertise in the editing of my manuscript.

Miriam Woods skillfully designed this book and guided it deftly through its production stages.

Jacob Behrman of Behrman House was a valued counselor and lent his expertise together with that of his talented staff.

I am personally indebted to all the artists for their understanding, warmth, and graciousness, and for the privilege of enjoying their friendship.

I express my gratitude to all of the above and to the congregation of Beth El Synagogue for their confidence in placing the direction of this work in my hands, and for giving me the opportunity to fulfill this wonderful mission.

Stanley I. Batkin is a native New Yorker and an alumnus of New York University. He and his wife, the former Selma Loinger, reside in New Rochelle, New York; they have two children and five grandchildren.

Mr. Batkin is active in many civic, cultural, educational, financial and religious organizations, and serves on twenty governing boards. As a result of his work at Beth El Synagogue, he is now a consultant on synagogue architecture. In addition to his photography in this book, he has won an international photography contest in London, England, and his work has been recognized in many other areas. He is a specialist in genealogy where he has traced his family back to the seventeenth century, and is an expert in the field of packaging holding several United States patents for improvements in this field. Mr. Batkin is the president of Universal Folding Box Co., Inc., of Hoboken, New Jersey.

INDEX

The type face used throughout this book is Electra,

designed by W. A. Dwiggins. Composition, printing—other

than color plates—and binding were done by

Hamilton Printing Company, Rensselaer, New York.

Design by Miriam Woods.

Two thousand copies have been issued, five hundred

of which have been numbered and signed by the author.